KRISTEN PARKER

The Thorn-Bound Heart

First edition

This book was professionally typeset on Reedsy.
Find out more at reedsy.com

Contents

One

The Heart's First Thorn

The moonlight spilled through the dense canopy, casting long, silver fingers across the forest floor. Liora walked through the woods with the grace of one accustomed to the whispers of nature, her every step quiet as the world around her held its breath. The air was thick with the scent of pine and moss, mingling with the faint sweetness of earth after rain. But something was different tonight— something that made the leaves rustle in a way that wasn't quite right, that made the shadows seem longer and more twisted than they should be.

Liora pressed a hand to her chest, feeling a flutter beneath her ribs, sharp and sudden, like the prickle of a thorn brushing against her skin. It was the third time today, this strange pain that gnawed at her, subtle yet persistent, a constant reminder of something she couldn't quite grasp. Her heart was restless, its rhythm erratic, and each time it pulsed, the sensation grew stronger, deeper, as though it were trying to speak to her, to tell her something.

She paused, glancing around the clearing, her breath quickening. The forest was silent now, unnervingly so, and she could have sworn she felt eyes upon her. But when she turned, there was nothing—only trees, dark and impenetrable, their branches reaching out like skeletal fingers.

The air shifted then, growing colder, the faintest whisper of movement stirring the underbrush to her right. Liora stiffened. She wasn't alone.

A low growl echoed from the depths of the forest, primal and guttural. Her heart skipped a beat, and she instinctively stepped back, her hand reaching for the pouch of herbs at her waist. She didn't know what it was, but she could sense the danger lurking in the darkness. Every nerve in her body screamed at her to flee, but the pull in her chest—the pain, the ache—kept her rooted to the spot.

Then, from the shadows, a figure emerged. Tall, broad-shouldered, cloaked in darkness. At first, Liora thought it was a shadow of the trees, another trick of the moonlight. But as it stepped forward, she saw him—his presence more real, more solid than anything in the forest around her.

The man was regal, a figure carved from the very essence of the night itself. His hair, as dark as the midnight sky, cascaded over his shoulders in thick waves. His eyes—piercing, sharp—locked onto hers with an intensity that stole the breath from her lungs. A strange recognition flickered in her chest, followed by a sudden, overpowering urge to step closer, to bridge the distance between them.

But she didn't move.

The man's gaze softened for a moment, almost imperceptibly,

and Liora felt the first pang of unease. She had seen him before, though she didn't know how or where. It was as if the very air around her hummed with the weight of an unseen connection, one that had yet to reveal its purpose.

"Who are you?" she asked, her voice steady despite the rapid beat of her heart.

His lips curled into a faint, wry smile, though there was no humor in it. "A question better left unanswered, I fear."

Liora narrowed her eyes. "You're not from the village."

"No," he said, his voice low and rich like the growl of a distant storm. "I am far from home."

His eyes flicked toward the ground, and for a moment, Liora thought she saw a brief flash of something—anger, frustration, or maybe pain—cross his features. But it was gone as quickly as it came, replaced by the cold, impenetrable mask he wore.

"You shouldn't be here," Liora said, though the words felt strange in her mouth, as though they weren't hers to speak.

His gaze shifted, scanning the forest as if searching for something. Then, his eyes returned to her, locking on hers with a gaze so intense it felt as if he were seeing into the very depths of her soul.

"I could say the same to you," he replied, his voice soft but carrying a weight she couldn't ignore. "But it seems we are both bound by fate."

The words hit her like a physical blow, and for a heartbeat, the world seemed to tilt. The strange, throbbing pain in her chest flared to life again, sharp and jagged, and she gasped, stumbling back. Her vision blurred, and for a moment, she was consumed by the sensation of drowning—drowning in the weight of something unknown, something terrible.

The man took a step toward her, his presence filling the space between them. His hand, calloused and strong, reached out to steady her, but Liora recoiled instinctively, the air between them crackling with a strange tension.

"You should go," she said, her voice shaking despite her best efforts to remain composed. "Now."

He didn't move. "You feel it, don't you?" His voice was quieter now, almost a whisper, but it carried a force that made her heart tremble. "The pull. The ache."

Liora didn't answer, but her chest tightened in response. The pain was unbearable now, a hot flare of something that was both familiar and foreign. She didn't know what it was, only that it was pulling her toward him in a way she couldn't explain.

"You're cursed," she said, the words leaving her lips before she even realized she'd spoken them. They tasted like ash, bitter and wrong.

He didn't flinch, but there was something in his eyes—a flicker of recognition. "And so are you."

Liora shook her head, but the doubt lingered in her chest. She wasn't cursed. Not like him. She was a healer, a woman of the earth, connected to the world in ways most people couldn't comprehend. She healed others. She couldn't be cursed.

But the pain in her chest—this gnawing, insistent ache—was unlike anything she had ever felt before.

"I don't know what you're talking about," she said, her voice steady but her words faltering.

The man's gaze softened again, and this time, she could see the sadness beneath the hardness, the deep sorrow that seemed to weigh him down like a heavy cloak. "You will," he said, his voice barely a whisper.

The silence stretched between them, thick with tension, and

then he spoke again, his words slow and deliberate.

"Liora, the curse that binds us… it is more than just a bond of fate. It is a bond of death."

The words struck her like a lightning bolt, and for the first time since she had encountered him, fear began to creep into her bones. Death? She didn't understand, couldn't understand, but the dark pull in her chest only grew stronger, more insistent.

The man took a step back, his gaze never leaving hers. "And no matter how far we run from it, no matter how much we fight it, it will find us. And when it does… you will feel it in your heart."

Liora stumbled back, her breath coming in quick, shallow gasps. The pain was unbearable now, a crushing weight in her chest that threatened to steal the air from her lungs. She closed her eyes, trying to block it out, but it was no use. It was there, a constant reminder that she was tied to him in a way she couldn't understand.

When she opened her eyes again, he was gone, melted into the shadows of the forest as though he had never been there at all.

But Liora could feel him. She could feel the weight of his presence lingering in the air, in the very bones of the earth beneath her feet.

And in her heart.

The curse had begun. And it would not let her go.

The forest stood still, unnaturally so, as if it too were holding its breath, waiting for something to happen. Liora stood there, heart hammering in her chest, the pain a constant throb, a reminder of the curse she didn't understand. Her legs felt unsteady beneath her, like the very earth was shifting, pulling away from her. She glanced around, her breath shaky, but the man—*Thorne*—was gone. The shadows had swallowed him whole, leaving no trace.

But the pain. The pressure in her chest was no longer a mere throb. It was a *force*, a pull that reached down into her very soul, tugging her toward something—or someone. Liora stumbled backward, her hand brushing against the rough bark of a nearby tree, grounding herself, as if the earth could anchor her to reality.

She closed her eyes and took a steadying breath, trying to calm the panic rising in her throat. She had to regain control. The world was spinning, and she was caught at its center, a helpless passenger. She pressed her palm against her chest, as if that might ease the relentless pulse that was beginning to echo in her ears, filling her with an odd mixture of dread and longing.

Her mind raced, the questions piling up, each one louder than the last. What had Thorne meant by the curse? Why had she felt that strange, unmistakable connection to him? She was a healer. She had studied the ancient texts, learned from her elders, felt the pulse of magic in the earth. But this… this was something beyond her understanding. The pain, the pull—those weren't just the echoes of magic. They were the harbingers of something far darker.

Liora's breath faltered. *"Liora, the curse that binds us… it is more than just a bond of fate. It is a bond of death."*

His words rang in her ears, a haunting refrain that refused to let go. Death. The very idea of it seemed absurd. She had spent her life bringing healing to the wounded, mending the broken, easing the suffering of others. Death was the one thing she could never abide. And yet, here it was, looming over her like a shadow she couldn't escape.

She had to find him. She had to understand what he meant—what this curse truly was.

But as she turned to leave, the sound of movement reached her ears—a low, echoing rustle, barely audible above the whisper of the wind. Her heart skipped. A sense of foreboding washed over her, urging her to flee, to retreat back to the village where she was safe. But the pull in her chest—the ache—was stronger than her fear. It was as though the earth itself was calling to her, urging her to follow it. To find him.

Liora took a deep breath, steeling herself against the fear that threatened to overwhelm her. She had to keep moving. She had to understand.

Her feet carried her deeper into the woods, the path winding and narrowing, shadows growing darker with every step. The moon above was hidden now, veiled by a veil of clouds that seemed to press down, suffocating the light. The forest felt alive in a way it never had before. The trees stretched their limbs like sentinels, reaching toward her, their branches creaking as though they were whispering secrets. The wind stirred the leaves, sending a chill through the air, and Liora shivered involuntarily. It wasn't the cold that made her shiver, though. It was something else, something far more unsettling.

A sudden rustle broke the stillness, and Liora froze. Her pulse quickened, her senses sharpening. She wasn't alone. She could feel it—something was watching her, moving just beyond the edges of her vision.

A shadow flickered across her path, too quick to be a deer or any of the other creatures she knew roamed these woods. Her breath caught in her throat.

And then, in an instant, it appeared.

A figure emerged from the shadows, tall and cloaked, his face hidden beneath the dark folds of a hood. Liora's breath hitched as her heart hammered in her chest. It was him—the man who had called himself Thorne.

But there was something different about him now. The air around him seemed heavier, darker, and his presence was far more commanding, as though the very night itself bent to his will. His eyes glowed faintly, a fierce, unnatural light that sent a shiver through Liora's spine.

He didn't speak at first. Instead, he watched her, his gaze intense, searching, as though weighing her very soul. She felt as if he could see right through her, as though her every thought, every secret, was laid bare before him.

Liora stood frozen, the pain in her chest now a constant, gnawing ache that only intensified as he drew closer. Her fingers tightened around the pouch of herbs at her waist, instinctively readying herself, though she wasn't sure what she was preparing for. He had done nothing but speak words, yet her entire body seemed to react to his presence as though he were a storm on the horizon—impending, unstoppable.

"You should not have come here," Thorne's voice was low, rich with an authority that made the hairs on the back of Liora's neck stand on end.

"I had to," she said, her voice steady despite the storm of emotions raging inside her. "I need to understand. I need to know what this curse is… and why it's pulling me to you."

A flicker of something—pain? Regret?—flashed across his face, though it disappeared as quickly as it had come. His jaw clenched, and his hand reached up to push the hood back from his face, revealing his sharp features, the hardened set of his jaw, and the dark, haunted look in his eyes.

"You don't want to understand," he said, his words heavy with finality. "You will wish you had never asked."

Liora stepped back, her heart pounding in her chest, the weight of his gaze pressing down on her. She had never been afraid of anything in the woods before. But this—*him*—this was different. This was not the man she had met earlier. This was something darker, something that carried death in its wake.

"I *have* to understand," she whispered, more to herself than to him.

Thorne's eyes softened, a brief flicker of what might have been empathy flashing in their depths. But it was quickly replaced by a coldness that made Liora's blood run cold.

"The curse binds us," he said slowly, as though the words themselves were a burden he had carried for far too long. "And it will bind you to me, as it has bound countless others before us."

Liora's breath caught. She had heard the legends. The tales of a cursed prince, doomed to bring ruin to the one he loved, doomed to destroy everything he touched. But hearing it from his lips—the truth of it—was something far more terrifying.

"Why me?" Liora asked, her voice barely a whisper.

Thorne's lips curled into a tight, bitter smile. "That… I do not know. But it will come for you, just as it came for me."

The forest seemed to grow colder as his words lingered in the air, and Liora's heart skipped a beat. The pull in her chest was unbearable now, a twisting knot of pain and dread that seemed to reach deeper with every passing second.

"I don't want this curse," she said, her voice trembling.

"You don't have a choice," Thorne replied, his voice dark, his eyes flashing with a pain she couldn't fathom. "No one does."

A silence stretched between them, thick with the weight of the curse, the unspeakable truth that hung between them like a blade waiting to fall.

And then, without another word, Thorne turned and disappeared into the shadows, leaving Liora standing in the silence, her heart pounding, her chest aching.

The curse had begun.

And there was no escaping it.

Two

Thorns of Fate

The winds of Rivenhold howled through the mountains, whipping the trees into a frenzy as if nature itself were trying to shake loose the secrets buried deep in the earth. Thorne stood at the edge of the cliff, his broad shoulders hunched against the biting cold. The pale moon cast long shadows over the jagged rocks below, but his gaze was fixed on the horizon, far beyond the forest that stretched out beneath him. The land seemed endless, as if it went on forever, and yet it felt smaller every day.

A pain gnawed at his chest, relentless and cruel, and for a fleeting moment, he wondered if the curse itself had taken root in his heart. It had been there since birth, whispering dark promises into his soul, but now, as his mind swirled with thoughts of her, it felt more like a weight—one he could never rid himself of. His connection to Liora had become something he could no longer ignore.

The curse had been passed down through the bloodline of the Halloway family for generations. It was said to be a punishment, an act of vengeance by the ancient gods. Every man of the family was doomed to carry the weight of it, cursed to fall in love with a woman whose death they would bring upon themselves. The heart would always beat for the one they loved, but in the end, it would be the blade of death they wielded, not the hands of healing.

Thorne had been running from this fate his entire life, trying to keep everyone at arm's length, to sever the ties of affection before they ever had a chance to grow. But the pull, the force of it, was undeniable.

"Thorne," a voice called from behind him, bringing him back to the present. He didn't need to turn around to know who it was. Cormac, his most trusted confidant and the only person who truly understood the weight Thorne carried. He had known Cormac since childhood. They had shared blood, sweat, and secrets, and in a world where Thorne had been taught to trust no one, Cormac was the one exception.

"Do you ever tire of this?" Thorne asked, his voice low, as he continued to gaze out over the darkened valley. "Standing at the edge, waiting for the inevitable to come crashing down?"

Cormac stepped up beside him, his heavy boots crunching against the frost-covered ground. "You should have come inside hours ago. The storm's coming. It's not wise to be out here, especially not tonight."

Thorne finally turned to face him. Cormac's face was hard, worn with years of battle and sorrow. But in his eyes, there was something softer—something that spoke of loyalty and brotherhood.

"I can't escape it, Cormac," Thorne said, his voice breaking.

He ran a hand through his dark hair, disheveled by the wind. "It's never been this strong before. The curse… the pull toward her. I thought I could keep my distance, but now… now I feel as though I am already tied to her."

"I see the change in you," Cormac replied, his voice thick with concern. "It's as though the curse has found a way to sink its claws deeper into you. Every time I see you, it's like a storm is brewing within you. And it's her, isn't it?"

Thorne's eyes hardened. He had never spoken of Liora to anyone. Not even Cormac, who had always been by his side. But the way the curse had begun to twist, to bind him in ways he couldn't explain, made it impossible to keep it to himself anymore.

"It's her," Thorne whispered, barely audible above the wind. "Liora… She's the one. I can feel it. I've tried to keep away. But every time I'm near her, it's as if the earth itself calls out to me. As if she's the center of everything I've ever known, and I'm being pulled closer, deeper into this madness."

He clenched his fists, his knuckles turning white. "I've tried. I've pushed people away, I've stayed far from her. But the curse… it's becoming stronger. Every time I see her, the need to protect her, to care for her… it's overwhelming. And it's *dangerous*, Cormac."

Cormac placed a hand on his shoulder, grounding him. "You know as well as I do that there's no escaping fate. The curse that binds your family to death… it was set long ago, before you or I even drew breath. But you've never known love like this, have you? Not like this, where you can feel the other person's heartbeat in your own chest."

Thorne's jaw clenched, his gaze returning to the distant horizon. "I haven't. But it's not just the pull, Cormac. It's the fact that it's already begun. I can feel it in her, too. The connection is *real*. The thorns of fate have already begun to twist around her heart, just like they did with me."

"Thorns?" Cormac asked, brow furrowed. "What do you mean?"

Thorne hesitated, the weight of his words threatening to suffocate him. The curse had always been something he had tried to ignore, to bury deep within himself, but now it was creeping into the very fabric of his reality, something he could no longer outrun.

"I've seen them," Thorne said finally. "I saw them on her palms when she touched the earth. Thorns… sharp, jagged, *alive* in a way that no human blood should carry. I know that the curse has begun to affect her, too. It has already taken root in her, Cormac. It's only a matter of time before it consumes us both."

Cormac's eyes widened in disbelief. "But how is that even possible? The curse should be bound to you, not her."

"It should be," Thorne replied grimly. "But something's changed. The power that binds us… it's no longer contained in my blood. It's reaching out to her, and I can feel it growing stronger with every passing day."

"There must be a way to stop it," Cormac said, determination flaring in his voice. "There's got to be a way to break the curse."

Thorne shook his head, his expression darkening. "I've tried every spell, every ancient text. I've consulted the seers, the shamans, the witches, all in an attempt to break free. But nothing works. This curse is older than time itself. It cannot be undone. It can only be passed on… and eventually, it will claim us both."

The words hung in the air like a death sentence, each one

heavier than the last. Thorne's chest tightened, and for the first time in years, he allowed himself to feel the weight of the truth he had always known: there was no escape. He would bring death to the one he loved. He would break her, just as his ancestors had broken their beloveds.

But the worst part—the part that gnawed at him every day—was that he wanted to love her. He wanted to hold her, to protect her, to feel the warmth of her skin beneath his touch. And in doing so, he knew he was only sealing her fate.

Meanwhile, in the heart of Rivenhold, Liora sat in her small cabin, the crackling fire casting flickering shadows against the stone walls. Her hands, trembling, hovered over a small bowl of water filled with herbs. She had been experimenting with her newfound power over the last few days, noticing strange things happening whenever she healed or touched something alive.

Her fingers brushed against a leaf, and instantly, she felt a sharp, stinging pain shoot through her palms. She gasped, pulling her hand back, and looked down at her skin.

Thorns. Tiny, jagged pricks of thorn-like growths had appeared along her palm, red and raw, as if they were pushing through her skin from the inside out. The sight made her stomach twist in both horror and fascination.

"What is this?" she whispered, her voice trembling.

The thorns seemed to pulse with an unnatural energy, writhing beneath her skin like living things, as if they had a will of their own. It was the same sensation she had felt when she touched Thorne—when their hands had brushed ever so briefly. The sensation had been fleeting, but in that moment, it had been as if the earth itself had trembled beneath her feet.

And now, here it was again. The thorns. The connection.

Liora stood up, pacing the room, trying to make sense of it. She had been raised to believe in the old ways, in the ancient powers that flowed beneath the earth, but nothing in her training had prepared her for this. She had no idea what was happening, but she knew it was tied to him.

Thorne.

She could feel him. Even now, in the stillness of her cabin, she could feel him. The pull was undeniable. It was as though her very soul recognized him. And worse, it *wanted* him.

The thorns on her hands were a warning. A warning of the danger she was in. The curse had already begun to bind them, and soon, it would be too late for either of them to break free.

Her palms burned, and the thorns grew more pronounced with each passing moment, sharp and cruel. She closed her eyes, trying to push through the panic that clawed at her chest, but the thorns would not let her go. They would not let her forget.

There was no escaping it. There was no escaping *him*.

And the curse had already begun.

Liora stood frozen, her palms throbbing as the thorns seemed to dig deeper into her skin, spreading like roots from the very core of her being. Her breath came in ragged gasps as she watched in horror, the tiny, jagged protrusions writhing with unnatural energy beneath the surface of her skin. She hadn't felt this before—not like this. Not with such force, such urgency. It was as if the earth itself was forcing its will upon her, as if something ancient, powerful, and unstoppable had taken root inside her.

The thorns weren't just in her hands. She could feel them deep inside her chest, twisting in the very fibers of her heart.

Her heartbeat pounded in her ears, a heavy, thunderous rhythm that resonated through every bone in her body. The connection to Thorne—the pull, the bond—it had intensified. And as much as she wanted to fight it, as much as she wanted to tear herself away from whatever dark force was tethering her to him, the truth was undeniable. It was happening. And it was happening with a ferocity she couldn't escape.

Liora staggered back, her hands clasped to her chest, trying to will herself into stillness. The thorns in her palms ached, but it wasn't just the physical pain. It was the crushing weight of what she knew was coming. *The curse.* It had already begun to weave its way into her, creeping through her veins like poison. And if what Thorne had said was true, if the curse was now bound to her—if she was part of this twisted fate—there would be no escaping the end.

She couldn't stop herself from thinking of him. Thorne. The way his eyes had held hers, as though they had seen through her very soul. As though she had somehow always been meant to meet him. But it couldn't be. She couldn't allow herself to be consumed by this—by him. There had to be another way. There had to be something she could do.

Liora turned abruptly, pacing the room, trying to make sense of everything. Her heart still pounded, her breath shallow. She hadn't told anyone about the strange connection between them. She hadn't confided in anyone about the way the curse had marked her, but now, she couldn't ignore it. It was impossible to ignore.

With trembling hands, she reached out to steady herself on the table, her fingers brushing the herbs she had been working with earlier. A small vial of healing salve tipped over, spilling its contents onto the table. But before she could move to clean it up, something strange happened. The salve, which had once been clear and pure, began to change, darkening before her very eyes. It swirled, taking on a murky, unnatural shade, like ink seeping into water. The air around her grew heavier, thicker. And in that moment, she felt a deep, pulsing throb in her chest, as though the very ground beneath her feet had started to hum with an ancient, primal power.

Liora recoiled, stepping back from the table. She didn't understand what was happening, but she knew one thing for sure: the curse was not just a curse. It was a force of nature, one that was already altering her in ways she couldn't control.

Her pulse quickened as she looked down at her hands. The thorns were still there, growing in intensity. Each small, sharp point seemed to pulse, as if they were alive, feeding off her energy. She winced as the pain flared again, hotter this time, a fiery surge of agony that made her knees weaken beneath her.

What am I becoming?

A sudden thought crossed her mind—something she hadn't considered before. She had always thought the curse was something that bound Thorne alone, something that followed his bloodline, but what if it wasn't? What if the curse could spread? What if it could latch onto anyone who came into contact with him, anyone who was close enough to be pulled into his orbit? She knew the stories—the legends of the prince who would destroy his one true love. But she hadn't known how deeply the curse ran, how easily it could entangle anyone who was even remotely tied to him.

Liora gasped, clutching her chest. The connection between them—it was real. The thorns in her hands were proof of it. She was already marked. And with every passing moment, she could feel the bond between them growing stronger, stretching further, until it threatened to swallow her whole.

Outside, the storm had grown fiercer, and the wind howled through the trees, rattling the windows of her small cabin. The fire crackled and hissed in the hearth, casting flickering shadows on the walls. Liora felt the strange, oppressive energy that surrounded her—something beyond the storm, beyond the physical world. The thorns in her palms seemed to respond to it, vibrating with an eerie pulse, and she closed her eyes, her heart racing.

I need to see him again.

The thought was immediate, sharp, undeniable. She could feel him, even now, somewhere out there in the storm. The pull was magnetic, insistent, calling her toward him. Despite everything, despite the curse and the danger it promised, she knew she couldn't resist. Not anymore.

With a deep breath, Liora grabbed her cloak from the back of the chair and threw it around her shoulders. She would find him. She would confront this curse head-on, even if it meant walking into the very heart of danger.

Thorne's thoughts were a tempest of their own, each one crashing violently against the next as he moved through the castle's dark halls. His footsteps echoed against the cold stone walls, each one feeling like a final countdown, an irreversible march toward the end. He had spent so many years trying to avoid this—trying to outrun the curse that had plagued his bloodline for generations. But now, now that Liora was in his life, it was as if fate had drawn the lines too close, as though he had no choice but to step right into its embrace.

He had retreated to his chambers, seeking solace in the solitude of his own mind, but the thoughts of her had been too overwhelming. Every time he closed his eyes, he saw her face, felt the warmth of her presence, heard the beating of her heart. And with that, the pain—the agony of knowing what he would ultimately bring to her.

She would die. It was inevitable.

Thorne's hand curled into a fist, his nails biting into his palms. The curse had always been a whisper, something in the background of his life. But now it was a roar, deafening and inescapable. The pull between them was too strong, and he couldn't ignore it anymore. He had tried. He had kept his distance. But it wasn't just the curse that bound him to her now—it was something deeper, something that went beyond blood or fate.

He heard the soft creak of the door, and before he could turn around, he felt her presence. Her scent, fresh and wild, filled the room, and his heart stumbled in his chest.

"Liora," he breathed, barely recognizing the rawness in his voice. She stood in the doorway, her face illuminated by the dim light of the fire in the hearth. There was a fire in her eyes, a spark of determination that matched the storm swirling outside.

Her hands—bare and trembling—were at her sides, and the thorns were still there, dark and sharp. He could feel them, even now, even from across the room. It was as if they were a physical manifestation of the bond between them.

"I couldn't stay away," she whispered, her voice quiet but steady. "I need to understand. I need to know what's happening to me. To us."

Thorne's chest tightened. He wanted to tell her to leave, to run far away and never look back. But he couldn't. He *wouldn't*.

"Liora…" His voice faltered, but he forced the words out. "This is dangerous. You can't… you don't understand the consequences."

Her gaze never wavered, and she took a step closer. "I don't care about the consequences. I need to know the truth."

And in that moment, as she stepped into his world, as the thorns between them reached their full bloom, Thorne knew—no matter how hard he tried to fight it—there was no turning back.

Three

The Heart's Cry

T he night was restless, with clouds churning in the sky like the twisting, writhing of a great serpent. Liora could feel the weight of it, the pressure in the air, as though the world itself were holding its breath. She stood at the edge of the forest, the wind howling through the branches, tugging at her cloak, and her thoughts were just as tangled, chaotic, and storm-tossed.

Her palms burned, as they had every day for the last week, the thorns a constant reminder of something she couldn't escape. The more she tried to ignore them, the more pronounced they became, growing in size and intensity with each passing hour. There was no relief, no peace. Every time she touched something, whether it was the rough bark of the trees or the smooth surface of water, the thorns dug deeper, as though they were pulling from her energy, from the very core of who she was. The pain was sharp, agonizing, but it was the way the thorns seemed to *live*—twisting and pulsing beneath her skin—that terrified her most.

She closed her eyes, pressing her hands to her chest, as though she could force them away. Her breath came quick, each inhale sharp with fear. *What is happening to me?*

The answer had been elusive, slipping through her fingers like smoke. She had gone to the village healers, seeking counsel, but none had been able to explain the growing power within her, nor the dark bond that had begun to tether her to Thorne. None of them had seen the thorns. None of them had felt the way her very soul seemed to cry out whenever she was near him.

The pull was undeniable, and yet she was terrified of it. Terrified of the man who had become a stranger in her life, yet whose presence seemed to dominate every thought, every feeling. He was the source of the curse, of the power that she could neither understand nor control.

And yet, despite the fear, despite the dread that clenched her heart every time she thought of the inevitable tragedy, there was a part of her that *wanted* him. A part of her that yearned for him, even as she knew that yearning would lead to her own destruction. She could feel it in her bones. The curse would claim her, just as it had claimed those before her.

Tonight, she couldn't deny it any longer. She needed answers. And the only place she could go for them was the oracle.

The oracle of Rivenhold was an ancient being, as old as the land itself. It was said that the oracle had the power to see into the future, to peer into the threads of destiny that wove through the hearts of all living creatures. But the oracle was not a being that gave answers easily. It spoke in riddles and cryptic warnings, and many who sought it left with more questions than they had come with.

Still, it was her only hope.

Liora's heart raced as she walked deeper into the forest, her footsteps soft on the damp earth. The path was narrow, winding through dense thickets of bramble and low-hanging branches that seemed to whisper in the wind. The trees were ancient here, their trunks gnarled and twisted, their roots sinking deep into the earth. The deeper she went, the more she felt the weight of the forest, the more the air seemed to thicken, as though it was alive with ancient power.

The oracle's dwelling was hidden from mortal eyes, a place where the veil between the physical world and the spirit realm was thin. Only those who were destined to find it could see it. And tonight, Liora's heart told her that she was destined to find it.

She emerged into a clearing, where the moonlight bathed a small stone temple in pale silver. The air was cool and still, the only sound the rustling of leaves in the wind. The temple itself was simple but imposing, its stone walls covered in ivy, its roof crowned with symbols of forgotten deities. There was a silence here that was almost holy, as if time itself had paused to observe.

Liora stepped forward, her breath steadying as she approached the temple's entrance. Her hand brushed against the ancient stones, the cool surface sending a shiver through her body. She paused before the threshold, gathering the courage to step inside.

The oracle waited for her, as it always had, in the heart of the temple. But she could not see it—not until she crossed the threshold. The moment she did, the air around her seemed to shimmer, and a figure appeared before her, clothed in flowing robes that gleamed like moonlight. The face was obscured by a veil, but Liora could feel the weight of its gaze, as though the oracle could see straight into her soul.

"You have come," the oracle's voice was low, its tone a mixture of sorrow and knowing. "I knew you would."

Liora swallowed hard, her voice trembling. "I need to understand. The thorns in my hands… the bond I share with him. Why has this curse marked me?"

The oracle was silent for a long time, the air thick with anticipation. Then, it spoke again, its voice like the rustling of dry leaves, soft and ancient.

"The curse is not yours alone. It was laid upon him first, and it has found you now, for you are the one who is meant to end it. But the ending will not come without cost."

Liora felt her chest tighten. "Cost? What do you mean?"

The oracle raised a hand, its fingers skeletal and long, pointing toward the moon above. "The curse is a burden, passed down through the ages. A bond forged in love, and sealed in death. You, Liora, are the key. The curse has claimed his heart, and now it claims yours. But love cannot break it. Only sacrifice can. Only in the moment of death can the bond be severed."

The words struck Liora like a physical blow, and she staggered back, her breath coming in quick gasps. "You're saying… I will die?"

The oracle's veiled face seemed to shift, its features unreadable. "You will die, but you will also live. The end of the curse will be the end of both of you—if you choose it. But you may also break free. You may choose to walk away, to sever the bond, to leave him behind. But in doing so, you will lose everything."

Liora's heart beat loudly in her chest, the pounding rhythm filling her ears. "But I can't… I can't just leave him. Not after everything. He—he is the only one who understands me. The only one who knows what this feels like."

The oracle was still, its silence stretching long and oppressive. "You must decide, child. The curse will not wait. And neither will he."

Liora's mind spun with the weight of the oracle's words. The pull between her and Thorne was too strong, too deep to ignore. She could feel it in every fiber of her being, the connection that was binding her to him. But the price—the price was unimaginable. Could she really choose between him and her own life? Could she truly end it all, sacrifice herself for the sake of the curse?

"I don't understand," she whispered, her voice barely audible. "How do I break it? How do I save us both?"

The oracle's voice was heavy with sorrow as it spoke its final words.

"There is no saving both of you. One must die for the other to live."

The words hung in the air, a cold, unyielding truth that threatened to crush her under its weight. Liora's breath caught in her throat, and she could feel her chest constricting. She had always known the curse was a tragedy, but hearing it spoken aloud, knowing that her love for Thorne could only end in one of their deaths—it was unbearable.

The oracle's figure began to fade, its presence dissolving into the air like mist. "The heart must choose. But remember, the heart is the first to break."

Thorne paced in the shadows of his castle, his mind a tumult of frustration and fear. The curse was tightening its grip on him, the pull toward Liora growing stronger with each passing day. He could feel it now, a tangible presence, like a weight pressing down on his chest. Every time he tried to push her away, to keep her safe, it was as though the curse retaliated, pushing them closer together, as if mocking his efforts.

He had seen the way her eyes had darkened when he was near. She could feel it too, couldn't she? The way the earth seemed to hum when they were in the same space. The way the air crackled between them. But he didn't know how much longer he could keep up this façade of distance. The more he tried to shield her from the curse, the more he knew he was only condemning them both.

He stopped at the window, staring out into the night. The storm had passed, but the feeling of dread remained, hanging in the air like a curse that refused to lift. And then, he felt it. A tug. A pulse. He could feel her—Liora—somewhere out there, moving toward something, toward a fate he couldn't control.

He could sense that she was on the verge of discovering something, something that would change everything. The very thought of it made his heart race. The curse was pushing her toward a truth, and he feared it was a truth they were both too afraid to face.

Liora was searching for answers. And when she found them, Thorne knew there would be no escaping what came next.

Liora stood in the temple's clearing, her heart racing as the weight of the oracle's words settled over her like an unshakable fog. She barely noticed when the figure of the oracle disappeared, its ethereal presence fading like smoke in the wind. The forest around her seemed darker now, as if the trees themselves had closed in, pressing upon her shoulders with the burden of the truth she had just learned.

One must die for the other to live.

The words echoed in her mind, each repetition adding to the heaviness that hung in the air. She clenched her fists at her sides, trying to steady herself, but the thorns in her palms only made it worse. The sharp, fiery pain seared through her skin once more, and she gasped, squeezing her eyes shut against the agony. Her body had become an unwilling battleground, her hands a reflection of the curse that was clawing at her from within, rooting deeper and deeper into her soul.

Her heart ached, not just from the physical pain, but from the deeper sorrow that the oracle's words had unleashed. *One must die.* How could she make that choice? How could she choose between herself and Thorne, between her love for him and the knowledge that his very existence threatened her life?

But even as that thought settled in her chest, she knew the truth: *she couldn't walk away from him.* Every fiber of her being cried out for him. The connection between them was too strong, too undeniable, to ignore. The pull of their fates was as much a part of her now as her own heartbeat.

Her breath quickened as the tension in her chest mounted, the thorns in her hands growing sharper with each passing second. She couldn't ignore them anymore. She couldn't pretend that everything would simply resolve on its own. The curse had already marked her, and it was only a matter of time before she lost control.

Liora turned toward the forest path, her heart hammering in her chest. She needed to return to the village. She needed to *do something*—anything—to try and make sense of the storm that was brewing inside her.

Her mind, however, kept circling back to Thorne. To him.

Thorne stood on the balcony of his castle, his eyes scanning the horizon, searching the darkened woods for a sign of Liora. He had felt the sudden pull of the connection between them earlier, and it had nearly driven him to madness. But he couldn't let her get too close—not now, not when the curse was so tightly wound around them both. The more he tried to shield her from the danger, the more it seemed to consume them both.

One must die for the other to live.

The words the oracle had whispered to him seemed to echo through his very being, like a death sentence that hung over them both. He couldn't escape it. He had tried for years, had distanced himself from everyone he loved, hoping that by keeping them at arm's length, he could avoid the tragic fate that would inevitably befall him.

But Liora—she was different. She had become the center of everything.

Her voice, her presence, haunted him, even when she wasn't near. He felt as though she were with him always, even in the moments when he was alone with his thoughts. Her laughter, her warmth, the way she looked at him with such trust—he knew what that trust meant. And yet, the more he allowed himself to feel it, the tighter the curse tightened its grip on him.

He had thought he could keep her safe. He had thought he could distance himself, push her away, but now he knew. It was no use. The curse was a force that would never be denied.

Thorne turned, his mind racing. He had to find her. He had to talk to her. To explain what was happening, to tell her the truth about the curse—about the price they both had to pay.

He strode quickly through the halls, his steps echoing in the empty corridors. His thoughts were a blur, each one flashing with uncertainty and dread. How could he protect her from this? How could he shield her from the inevitability of what was to come?

The answer was clear. He couldn't.

Liora arrived at her cabin, the door swinging open with a creak as she stepped inside. The warmth of the fire that crackled in the hearth greeted her, but it did little to quell the coldness that had settled in her bones. Her fingers were numb from the thorns in her palms, and the ache in her chest was growing with each passing second.

She paced the room, her thoughts a storm that threatened to consume her. The weight of the oracle's prophecy pressed down on her, suffocating her with its clarity. But it was the thought of Thorne—the thought of him standing on the precipice of destruction—that filled her with the deepest dread.

How could she love him when love meant death? How could she protect him when she was the one who would destroy him?

The thorns in her hands flared again, the pain sharper this time, as if they were a physical manifestation of the anguish twisting within her. She gasped, staggering back, her breath coming in quick, shallow gasps. The thorns dug deeper, and for a moment, everything seemed to go dark, the world around her fading into a blur.

Then, suddenly, there was a knock at the door.

Liora's heart skipped a beat. She knew who it was before she even opened it. The pull between them had become undeniable. It was him.

She slowly crossed the room, her feet heavy as though she were walking through water. The door opened to reveal Thorne standing on the other side, his tall frame silhouetted against the dim light of the fire. His expression was unreadable, a mask of tension and uncertainty.

"I need to speak with you," he said, his voice low, almost strained.

Liora's breath caught in her throat as she looked at him. She could feel the thorns in her hands, the way they pulsed and throbbed with an energy that seemed to be feeding off their proximity.

"I know," she whispered. "I know everything."

Thorne's gaze darkened, his jaw tightening. He stepped into the cabin, his presence overwhelming, filling the small space with a strange sense of inevitability.

"You spoke to the oracle," he said, his voice thick with a mixture of fear and resignation. "You know what the curse means now. What it will do to us."

Liora nodded, her heart aching with the weight of the knowledge. She glanced down at her hands, her fingers trembling. "I know," she repeated. "One must die for the other to live. The curse... it's not something we can escape."

Thorne's face was unreadable, but there was a flicker of something in his eyes—something she couldn't name. "I've tried, Liora. I've tried to keep you safe. To push you away. But I've only made it worse."

Her eyes snapped to his, her voice rising in desperation. "What do you mean, *worse*? You've only made it worse by trying to keep me from you. By trying to protect me from what's happening."

Thorne stepped forward, closing the distance between them. His hand reached out to gently grasp her wrist, his fingers warm against the coldness of her skin. The thorns in her palms flared, sending a pulse of pain through her entire body. She gasped, her breath hitching as her heart pounded.

"I never wanted this for you," Thorne said, his voice raw. "I never wanted you to suffer for something that was never your fault."

"But it's happening," Liora whispered, the words heavy in her chest. "And we can't stop it. Can we?"

Thorne's gaze softened, but the sadness in his eyes was unmistakable. "I don't know. But I won't let you face it alone."

The air between them seemed to vibrate with the unspoken truth that neither of them could deny anymore. The curse was inescapable. The bond between them was too strong, too dangerous, to ignore. And in that moment, Liora knew that they were both bound to each other—not just by fate, but by something deeper, something that transcended the curse itself.

Her heart cried out in a way she couldn't explain, a sharp, desperate ache that surged through her chest. She looked into his eyes, seeing the same pain reflected in them. And for the first time, she realized the truth that the oracle had whispered to her.

They would never be able to escape this.

And whatever came next, they would face it together.

Four

The Forbidden Touch

The forest was quiet, unnervingly so. The trees stood like silent sentinels, their gnarled limbs stretched upward toward the sky, their leaves trembling in a soft, uneasy breeze. The air itself felt thick, as though something ancient and powerful stirred just beneath the surface of the earth, waiting for the right moment to rise.

Liora stood at the edge of the glen, her heart pounding in her chest. She could feel it—an undeniable pull toward the clearing, a force she could not resist. Every step she took seemed to draw her closer to something she could not name, something that burned in her veins, something that had been waiting for her since the moment her path had crossed with Thorne's.

Her fingers trembled as she brushed the leaves aside, stepping into the open space where the sunlight flickered through the dense canopy, casting sharp beams of gold onto the forest floor. She paused, the familiar weight of the thorns in her palms reminding her of the bond she shared with him. The connection was undeniable now, every touch, every brush of his skin against hers, like a fire igniting within her. The thorns, once small and barely noticeable, had grown into jagged, cruel shapes that seemed to burrow into her very soul.

He's here.

Liora didn't need to look around to know Thorne was nearby. The pull of the curse—the invisible thread between them— tugged at her heart like a rope drawn taut. It was becoming unbearable. She had tried to fight it, tried to push him away, but each time they were near, it became more difficult to ignore. The bond between them was too strong, too consuming. And she feared it would break her.

A sound broke the stillness of the glen, and Liora turned toward it, her breath catching in her throat.

There he was—Thorne, stepping out from the shadow of the trees, his tall figure casting a long, dark silhouette against the golden light. His eyes locked onto hers, and for a moment, neither of them moved, as if the world had stopped, leaving only the two of them standing in the center of it. The tension between them was palpable, charged with something unspoken, something that neither of them could ignore.

Thorne's jaw tightened as he took a step toward her, his gaze never wavering. Liora's pulse quickened, her hands tightening at her sides as if she could somehow stop the storm of emotions brewing within her. She opened her mouth to speak, but the words wouldn't come. Instead, she could only stand there, her heart racing as she felt the inevitable draw of his presence.

"Liora," he said, his voice rough with something that sounded like regret, or maybe fear. She couldn't tell. But it sent a tremor through her, a crack in the wall she had tried to build around her heart.

"I didn't want to find you like this," he continued, his words quiet but heavy. "I thought I could keep you safe, away from all of this… but it's too late now, isn't it?"

Liora swallowed hard, her throat tight. She wanted to tell him to stay away, to keep his distance, but the truth was, she didn't want him to. Every part of her cried out for him, for the connection they shared, despite the danger it brought.

"I… don't know how to fight this," she whispered, her voice barely audible, her eyes searching his for some answer. "It's growing stronger, Thorne. The curse, the bond between us… it's becoming too much."

Thorne's gaze softened, and for a fleeting moment, the hardness in his eyes faded. He reached out, his fingers brushing lightly against her arm, the touch barely a whisper of sensation. But in that instant, the world seemed to shift. A spark ignited between them, a surge of raw energy that coursed through their bodies, lighting them both on fire.

Liora gasped, her entire being flooded with a sudden rush of power. The thorns in her palms flared to life, digging deeper into her skin as if responding to the magic surging through her veins. She felt the pulse of the earth beneath her feet, the heat of the air around them, the electric charge in the very air they breathed. It was as if the world itself was reacting to their touch, to the bond that had become impossible to ignore.

Thorne recoiled slightly, his eyes wide with shock, but his hand remained on her arm, unwilling to pull away. Liora's breath came in ragged gasps as she struggled to control the wild surge of magic within her. She could feel it—feel the raw, untamed power that had always been a part of her, but now, unleashed in a way she had never experienced before.

The world seemed to bend around them, the air thickening, crackling with energy. And then, without warning, the ground beneath their feet shook, sending a jolt of fear through Liora's chest.

From the edge of the glen, shadows stirred—figures cloaked in darkness emerging from the trees. The scent of danger was thick in the air, and Liora's heart skipped a beat as she realized they were surrounded.

Thorne's hand shot to his sword, his body moving with the practiced grace of someone who had spent years in battle. "Get back," he ordered, his voice low and fierce. But Liora didn't move. She couldn't. The connection between them, the magic that had flared up between their touch, was still alive in the air, and she could feel it building inside her.

The first figure lunged forward, a shadowy blur, and Thorne's sword sliced through the air, meeting the figure with a sharp, metallic clash. But Liora didn't have time to focus on the fight. Her pulse was still racing, her hands still burning with the power that threatened to break free. She could feel it inside her, the magic that had been suppressed for so long, fighting to be set loose.

"Liora, stay back!" Thorne's voice was harsh, a command that should have been obeyed, but it was too late. The energy within her had already begun to build.

A scream tore from Liora's throat as her hands shot forward, the thorns in her palms flaring painfully. She didn't know what she was doing. She couldn't control it. The magic within her surged like a wave crashing against the shore, wild and untamed. A blinding light erupted from her palms, sending the attackers stumbling backward with the force of the blast.

Thorne shouted in warning as the light radiated outward,

consuming everything in its path. The air crackled with raw power, the ground trembling beneath their feet as if the very earth was responding to the chaos she had unleashed.

The attackers were knocked off their feet, some of them flying backward with a violent force, others collapsing to the ground in a dazed heap. Liora's vision blurred as the magic burned through her, the energy leaving her dizzy, her body trembling with the strain of wielding power she barely understood.

The glen was silent for a moment, save for the ragged sound of their breathing. The attackers were still, their forms motionless on the ground. But Liora could feel the weight of the power within her, still alive, still pulsing, like a heartbeat in the very air around them.

Thorne's voice was quiet, almost reverent as he stepped toward her, his gaze locked on her hands, where the thorns had grown even larger, more pronounced, their jagged edges glowing faintly with the magic that had just been unleashed. "You did that," he said, his voice thick with awe and something else—something she couldn't place. "You controlled it."

Liora looked down at her palms, the thorns now twisted, coiled, like serpents wrapped around her hands. They pulsed with an energy that was both terrifying and exhilarating. "I didn't mean to," she whispered, her voice trembling. "I couldn't stop it."

Thorne reached out, his fingers grazing her wrist, his touch sending a shock of energy through her. She felt the pull of it, the connection between them growing even stronger as their magic intertwined. But it was more than just magic. It was their fates, bound together, tugging at them, forcing them to acknowledge the truth they could no longer deny.

He stepped closer, his presence overwhelming, and for a moment, Liora thought he might kiss her, might give in to the pull between them. But the moment passed, and instead, he gripped her shoulders, his hands steadying her.

"Liora," he whispered, his voice low and urgent. "We can't keep running from this. From what we are. From what we're becoming. The curse… it's not just in our blood. It's in our very souls."

Liora's heart thudded painfully in her chest, and she could feel the weight of his words sinking in. The magic, the thorns, the bond between them—it was all part of something they couldn't control. Something bigger than either of them.

And yet, as she stood there, her body trembling with the aftermath of the magic that had just erupted from her, one thing was clear: They could no longer stay apart. The connection between them was a ticking time bomb. And neither of them knew when it would explode.

The moment stretched between them, thick with the weight of their shared realization. Liora could feel her heart hammering in her chest, the echoes of the magic still vibrating in the air, lingering like a pulse beneath her skin. Her hands, still trembling, clenched into fists as she fought to steady herself. The thorns, though smaller now, had not disappeared entirely. Instead, they seemed to writhe beneath her skin, responding to the chaos she had unleashed.

Thorne's eyes locked onto hers, and for a moment, the world around them seemed to blur, leaving only the two of them standing in the center of the glen, surrounded by the stillness of the aftermath. The bodies of their attackers were scattered on the ground, unmoving. The silence in the air was suffocating, but the tension between them was even more oppressive.

"Liora," Thorne breathed, his voice barely above a whisper. The sound of her name on his lips made her heart tighten, and she could feel the weight of everything that had led them to this point—everything that would follow.

The realization crashed down on her like a wave. The connection between them was no longer something she could ignore. The curse had drawn them together, but now, the magic had bound them in a way that she couldn't undo. And it terrified her. Every instinct screamed at her to run, to leave, to try and break free before it was too late. But the truth was that she couldn't. She *wouldn't*.

"I never wanted you to be part of this," Thorne said, his voice raw, his hand trembling as it reached out to touch her arm. His fingers brushed the exposed skin of her wrist, and the magic flared again, a heat that spread through her like wildfire. The thorns on her palms pulsed in rhythm with her heartbeat, and the pain was no longer just physical. It was something deeper—something that connected her to him in a way that was both unbearable and impossible to resist.

"I didn't ask for any of this either," Liora replied, her voice catching in her throat as she stepped back, her pulse racing. She could feel the pull of him even now, tugging at her heart. "But I can't stop it, Thorne. I can't stop what's happening between us."

He reached for her, his expression softening as his gaze dropped to her hands, where the thorns had grown even more pronounced. "It's too dangerous," he said, his voice low, the urgency clear in his tone. "You don't understand what this is. What it could mean. What we could become."

Liora shook her head, her chest tightening as the words hit

her like a blow. "I don't care what it means. I can't just pretend it doesn't exist, Thorne. It's part of me. Part of us."

She could see the conflict in his eyes—an agonizing mix of fear and something else, something she couldn't name. But it was there, deep within him, just beneath the surface. He wanted to push her away, to keep her safe, to protect her from the curse that had already taken root in both their hearts. But in doing so, he only drove them closer together.

Before Thorne could respond, a low growl cut through the silence, breaking the moment. The ground trembled again, a subtle vibration that hummed beneath their feet. Liora's eyes snapped toward the source of the sound—a rustling in the trees to the north. A dark figure emerged from the shadows, its form shifting like smoke in the fading light of the day. The figure was tall, its silhouette framed by the dense trees, and as it stepped into the glen, Liora's heart skipped a beat.

The figure was one of their attackers. But there was something different about this one. The cloak it wore was dark and tattered, as if it had been through countless battles. But more than that—there was an aura of malice around it, a presence that seemed to make the air grow colder, denser.

"Thorne Halloway," the figure hissed, its voice dripping with venom. "You've managed to escape us for far too long."

Thorne's hand went to the hilt of his sword, but Liora felt the familiar, electrifying surge of magic stirring within her once more. This time, it was stronger. Darker. The thorns in her palms pulsed as though they were alive, and she could feel the energy crackling within her, threatening to burst free once again.

"Liora," Thorne warned, his voice low, but she could hear the edge of desperation beneath it. "Stay back. This is not your fight."

But the magic within her surged with a force that could not be denied. The power was *hers*, and it was growing with every passing second. She felt it in her chest, a heavy weight that threatened to suffocate her. She didn't know how to control it, how to stop it. But she could feel it in her blood, in her very bones. This magic—it was *her*. And it was *him*. It was both of them, twisted together in a way that neither of them could ever escape.

The figure in front of them took a step forward, and the air seemed to grow colder still. "You should have stayed hidden, Prince. You should have stayed *gone*," it sneered, its eyes glowing with a sickly yellow light. "But now, you've brought her into the fold. Now, it's too late."

Liora felt the thorns tighten around her heart. She glanced at Thorne, seeing the grim determination in his eyes. He knew what was at stake. He knew what this meant. But even so, he had come for her. And now, they were both standing here, in the midst of a battle they had never wanted to fight, yet could never avoid.

Before either of them could react, the figure lunged, its hand raised as if to strike. But the moment it moved, Liora's instincts took over. Her hands shot out, and with a fierce cry, the magic within her exploded.

A wave of raw power erupted from her palms, a surge of energy that tore through the air like lightning. The force of it sent the figure stumbling backward, its cloak flapping wildly as it struggled to regain its balance. The ground beneath them cracked and split, trees snapping in half with the force of the magic she had unleashed.

Thorne's eyes widened as he took a step back, shielding

himself from the blast. But Liora didn't stop. The power was out of control, flooding her body, surging through every fiber of her being. She felt the magic coursing through her, the thorns in her palms burning as they reached their full potential.

"No!" Thorne shouted, his voice barely reaching her over the roar of the energy. "Stop!"

But it was too late. The magic had already taken over, and Liora could do nothing to stop it. She could feel the energy swirling around her, dark and potent, feeding off the connection she shared with Thorne. The force of it created a barrier of raw power between them and their enemies, but at the same time, it consumed her, pulling at the very essence of her being.

When the magic finally subsided, there was a silence that hung heavy in the glen, broken only by the sound of their ragged breathing. The figure that had attacked them was gone, disappeared into the shadows from where it had come, as if it had never been there at all.

Liora stood in the center of the glen, her body trembling, her heart racing. The thorns on her hands had nearly doubled in size, the jagged edges pulsing with the energy she had just released. Thorne stepped toward her, his expression a mixture of awe and fear.

"That… that power," he whispered, his voice hoarse. "It's *too much*, Liora. You can't control it."

Liora's breath caught in her throat as she realized the truth. The power inside her was growing—growing faster than she could understand. And with each surge, with each spark of magic that flared between them, she was becoming something more. Something she could not stop.

"I… I didn't mean to—" Liora began, but Thorne's hand

reached out, gently cupping her face, silencing her.

"You don't need to explain," he said softly. "But we need to leave here. They'll be back, and next time, they won't make it so easy."

Liora nodded, her heart heavy with the realization that they could no longer run from what they were. From what they had become.

And the most terrifying part of it all was that she knew the worst was yet to come. The thorns tightening around her heart weren't just a symbol of the curse. They were a reminder. A reminder that love—true love—could never be without its price. And their love was a ticking time bomb.

Five

The Thorned Choice

The kingdom of Rivenhold sprawled before them like a tapestry woven with the threads of history and magic. Its stone towers rose against the horizon, their peaks hidden by clouds, while the vast, ancient forest stretched on beyond the castle walls. The land itself seemed to carry a weight, a burden, as if it remembered the curse that had clung to its soil for generations. Every step Liora took seemed to echo with the knowledge that she was bound to this place, to Thorne, to the curse that would shape both their fates.

Liora's hands clenched at her sides, the thorns embedded in her palms pulsing in time with the beat of her heart. Every step felt heavier than the last, as if the weight of the world had settled on her shoulders. Beside her, Thorne walked with an intensity that mirrored her own—his jaw set, his eyes distant as he stared straight ahead. Neither of them spoke as they crossed the courtyard, the silence between them a chasm they couldn't seem to bridge.

Their destination loomed before them now—the tower of Zaran, the kingdom's greatest wizard. The man who had once been revered as the master of all arcane knowledge, the one who held the keys to the mysteries of Rivenhold's ancient magic. If anyone could provide the answers they so desperately sought, it would be him.

Thorne had insisted on coming with her. He had told her time and time again that he would not let her face the truth alone. But even as they neared the tower's entrance, the air between them crackled with tension. The curse, the magic that bound them together, had only grown stronger since their encounter in the glen. Every brush of their hands, every glance, seemed to set the world on fire. The thorns in Liora's hands flared at the thought of him, and the pain that accompanied it was a constant, gnawing reminder of what would come if they could not break free of this curse.

The heavy wooden door of the tower creaked open as they approached, revealing a dimly lit corridor lined with shelves stacked high with scrolls, tomes, and arcane relics. The air was thick with the scent of aged parchment, incense, and something else—something far more ancient, far more dangerous.

Zaran stood at the far end of the room, his back to them, his fingers delicately tracing the pages of an open book. He was a tall man, with long, silvered hair that fell to his waist, and his robe shimmered in the low light as if woven from the very stars themselves. His sharp features were pale, his eyes as dark and deep as the void, reflecting a wisdom that spanned centuries. He was the last of the old order, the only one who had dared to study the curse that had haunted the Halloway bloodline for generations.

Without turning, Zaran spoke. "You've come to seek the truth."

Thorne stepped forward, his voice low and measured, but there was an edge to it that spoke of his desperation. "We need your help. The curse… it's too strong. It's consuming us. Liora… she's connected to it. And every time we try to separate, the pain grows worse. Please, Zaran. Tell us how to stop it."

Zaran's hands stilled on the book, and he turned slowly, his eyes locking onto Thorne with an unsettling intensity. "The truth is a dangerous thing, Prince Halloway. You may not wish to hear it."

Liora felt a cold chill run down her spine at his words. She glanced at Thorne, but he said nothing, his expression unreadable. Zaran's gaze shifted to her then, and for a moment, she felt as though he were peering into her very soul. She wanted to look away, but she couldn't. His eyes seemed to draw her in, filling her with a sense of ancient power that made her feel small, insignificant in the grand scheme of things.

"You," Zaran said softly, "are the key to this curse. But you are also its downfall."

Liora's breath hitched at his words. "What do you mean?" she asked, her voice shaky with the weight of the question.

Zaran motioned for them to sit at the long, oak table in the center of the room, his fingers still lightly tracing the pages of the book. As they settled into their seats, the wizard began to speak, his voice low and filled with an unsettling calm.

"The curse that binds you is not of this world," Zaran began. "It is ancient, older than the kingdom itself. It was created by the gods as punishment for your ancestors' betrayal. Each man in the Halloway line is born with this curse, doomed to fall in love with the one who will ultimately destroy them. But the true nature of the curse was hidden, even from those who sought to break it."

Liora's heart raced as she listened, her thoughts spinning. She had always known that the curse was linked to Thorne, to the bloodline he carried, but to hear the weight of it spoken aloud—*to hear it confirmed*—was something entirely different. She glanced at Thorne, whose face was pale, his hands clenched tightly in his lap. The burden of his family's fate seemed to crush him in that moment, and for the first time, Liora saw him not as the prince, not as the man who had fought to keep her safe, but as a person utterly trapped in the chains of destiny.

Zaran continued, his voice growing darker. "The bond between you and Thorne was meant to be broken when you met. But something has changed. The curse has not only bound your fates together—it has tied your hearts so tightly that it has become a part of your very essence. You cannot be free of it, not without great sacrifice. The only way to break the curse is to sever your bond, to cut the connection between you completely."

Liora's breath caught in her throat. "Sever the bond? But… that would mean—"

"Yes," Zaran interrupted, his voice unwavering. "It would mean death. For one of you, at least. The magic is woven so tightly around you both that to separate would tear you apart. The curse is insidious, and it feeds on the love that binds you. If you attempt to break the connection, it will consume you both."

Liora's hands trembled, the thorns in her palms throbbing with pain as Zaran's words sank in. She had feared this. She had known, deep down, that the bond between her and

Thorne was too strong to be ignored. But the thought of it—of losing him, of losing herself—was a terror that she had never imagined.

Thorne stood suddenly, his fists clenched at his sides. "There has to be another way," he growled, his voice filled with anguish. "There has to be something we can do to fight it. We can't just give up. We can't… I can't lose her. I won't."

Zaran's gaze softened, though there was no pity in it. "I understand your desire to fight, Prince. But this is not a battle you can win. The curse is not something to be conquered by will or strength. It is an immutable law, a force that exists beyond the reach of mortal men. The only way to survive is to sever the bond. But know this—one of you will die in the process. And you cannot know in advance who that will be."

Liora looked at Thorne, her heart aching at the tortured expression on his face. She could see the weight of the decision pressing down on him, the same fear she felt reflected in his eyes. How could they choose? How could they possibly make that decision, knowing that one of them would be lost forever?

The room fell silent. Zaran's words hung in the air like a death sentence, suffocating them both. Finally, Thorne spoke, his voice thick with emotion. "You're telling us that the only way to survive this curse is to *kill* one of us?"

Zaran nodded solemnly. "The curse was never meant to be broken. It was designed to bring ruin to the Halloway line. The gods made it so that only through destruction could the bond be severed. Only by death can you be free."

Liora's eyes burned with tears, but she refused to let them fall. She looked at Thorne, her heart breaking with the weight of what had been said. She could feel the tension in his shoulders, the way he was trying to hold himself together, to fight for her, for them. But there was nothing left to fight. The curse was too powerful, too far-reaching. There was no way out.

"I won't let you die for me," Liora said, her voice trembling. "I won't be the one to end this. If anyone is going to sacrifice themselves, it should be me. You have too much to live for, Thorne. You deserve to live. You deserve freedom from this."

Thorne's face darkened, his anger flaring. "And what about you, Liora? What about your life? Do you think I could live without you? I won't lose you. Not like this."

Tears welled in Liora's eyes, but she fought them back, the pain of their situation threatening to consume her. "I will protect you, Thorne," she whispered, her voice barely a breath. "No matter the cost. I will do whatever it takes to free you from this curse. Even if it means… even if it means giving up my life."

Thorne took a step toward her, his face a mask of sorrow and fury. "Don't say that. You are not going to die for me. *I* will not let you."

Liora shook her head, her heart breaking at the look in his eyes. "We have no choice, Thorne. We never did."

Zaran's voice cut through the tension. "You are both at a crossroads. And the path you choose will decide your fates. But know this: love is not always enough to save you. Sometimes, the only way to survive is to let go."

Liora felt the weight of his words settle over her like a shroud. The curse had always been a shadow hanging over them, but now, in this moment, it had become something else. It was not just a punishment—it was a decision they would have to make. A choice between love and survival.

But as Liora looked at Thorne, the man she had come to love more than life itself, she knew there could be no choice. There was no way she could ever walk away from him. No matter the cost.

"I will protect you," she whispered again, the words a vow, a promise she would keep. "Even if it kills me."

Thorne reached for her then, his fingers trembling as they brushed her cheek. His touch was gentle, despite the storm raging within him. "I don't want to lose you, Liora."

"I know," she whispered, tears finally spilling down her cheeks. "I know."

The room seemed to close in around them, the walls pressing inward with the weight of the decision they had yet to make. Liora stood there, trembling, caught between her love for Thorne and the unbearable truth of the curse that bound them together. Each moment felt like an eternity, each heartbeat a reminder of the magic coursing through her veins, the thorns embedded in her palms like a cruel testament to their shared fate.

Thorne's hand still lingered on her cheek, his touch gentle but firm, as if he were trying to anchor her to him, to this world, to *them*. But she could feel the weight of his sorrow, the suffocating sense of helplessness that seemed to radiate from him. He didn't want to let her go, and neither did she. But how could they live with the curse? How could they be together when it would ultimately destroy them both?

Liora pulled away from him slowly, her heart heavy with the grief that was already beginning to take root. "We can't keep fighting against this," she whispered, though the words felt like a dagger to her own soul. "No matter how much we want to. It's not just the magic, Thorne. It's everything. The curse has already woven us together in a way we can't undo. The only way to break free is for one of us to die."

She felt his gaze on her, the pain in his eyes a reflection of her own. "I *won't* let you sacrifice yourself for me," he said, his voice a low growl of desperation. "I can't live with that. I won't survive it."

Liora turned to face him fully, her hands shaking at her sides. The thorns in her palms seemed to writhe with an energy all their own, as though they were responding to the intensity of their emotions. "But you're already living with this curse, Thorne. You've lived with it your whole life. You've carried it alone. I won't let you continue to suffer because of me. I won't be the one who drags you into this darkness any longer."

Her voice broke on the last words, and Thorne took a step toward her, his expression fierce, determined. "I *will* suffer for you. I will endure whatever it takes to keep you safe, Liora. I won't—"

"Don't," she interrupted, her voice shaking. "Don't make promises you can't keep. This isn't about us anymore. This is about breaking the curse. And if one of us has to die, then let it be me. It's the only way for you to be free."

Thorne's face twisted with agony, his eyes flashing with fury and helplessness. "I can't lose you, Liora. I can't lose you like this. I won't watch you die for me."

The intensity of his words made her heart clench painfully. She had never seen him so vulnerable, so raw, and it made her love him even more. But it also made the reality of their situation that much harder to bear.

Liora reached out, her fingers brushing lightly over the thorns that marred her hands, the pain sharp and unrelenting. She let out a soft sigh, staring down at the cruel reminder of the bond they shared. "The curse isn't just about magic, Thorne.

It's about *fate*. The gods themselves made sure we would never have peace. They designed this to destroy us."

She turned away from him, unable to meet his gaze any longer. "I can't live with knowing that you're suffering because of me. But if one of us is going to die, then I'll make that sacrifice. I'll protect you—*I will protect you, Thorne*, no matter the cost."

Her voice cracked on the last words, and she felt the weight of the decision settle like a stone in her chest. Thorne's eyes were on her, but she couldn't look at him now. She couldn't bear to see the pain reflected in his face.

Zaran, who had been standing silently at the far side of the room, his hands folded over the ancient book, spoke again, his voice cutting through the thick air. "The choice you face is not an easy one. It never was meant to be. But understand this: there are no true victories here. Either you sever the bond, and one of you will die, or you embrace the curse, knowing it will consume you both in the end. This is the curse of your bloodline. And it will never let you go."

Liora felt a shiver race down her spine at the weight of the wizard's words. The idea of choosing death seemed impossible, unfathomable. Yet she knew, in her heart, that it might be the only way for them to escape the inevitable doom the curse had set for them.

"I understand," she whispered, though her voice was barely audible. "But I will protect Thorne. Even if it means losing everything."

Thorne's breath hitched at her words, his chest rising and falling with the rhythm of his agitation. He took a step closer to her, his eyes filled with sorrow and determination. "No, Liora. I won't let you do this. I love you, and I will fight for you until my last breath. We'll find another way. There *has* to be another way."

But his words rang hollow in Liora's ears. There was no other way. She had known it for a long time. The curse had already set its roots in her heart. And if they couldn't break it, then it would be the end of them both. It was either death now, or destruction later.

The weight of it all felt suffocating. She couldn't bear the thought of losing him. But she couldn't bear the thought of him living with the curse either.

"Thorne," she said quietly, her voice trembling as she turned to face him. She reached for his hand, the thorns biting into her skin, and she ignored the pain. "I love you. But I won't let you die because of me."

He closed his eyes at the words, a pained expression crossing his face. "Liora…" he whispered, his voice breaking. "You don't know what you're asking. I can't live without you. I just *can't*."

She took a deep breath, her heart breaking with every word. "You have to live, Thorne. You have to survive. You have to find a way to move on. And I will be with you. In some way… I will be with you."

She could see the conflict in his eyes, the sharp pain, and the growing realization that this was the end. There was no turning back. The curse had marked them both, and no matter how much they fought, the outcome was inevitable.

Liora swallowed hard, trying to steady her breath, her hands trembling as she clasped his fingers tighter. "Promise me that you'll live. Promise me that you'll fight for your freedom, even if I'm not there to stand by your side."

Thorne's voice was thick with emotion, his grip on her hand tightening as he spoke, his words like a quiet plea. "I promise you, Liora. But don't ask me to let you go. Don't make me choose between you and everything else."

Tears welled in Liora's eyes, but she pushed them back. "I'm asking you to choose, Thorne. I'm asking you to survive. For me."

The room was silent for a long moment, save for the sound of their breathing. Zaran stood in the corner, watching them with a mixture of quiet sorrow and detached understanding. He had seen this before. He had seen the broken hearts of those who tried to defy the gods, who tried to fight fate. And he knew that no matter what choice they made, it would come at a terrible cost.

Liora felt her chest tighten, her heart aching with the weight of her decision. She wanted to run, to escape, to fight for something—anything—but she knew, deep down, that there was no escaping the curse. Not now. Not ever.

And so, she made a vow, one she would carry with her into the darkest corners of her soul: *I will protect you, Thorne. No matter the cost.*

Her heart cracked with the finality of it, and though she knew what she was about to do would destroy her, she also knew that it was the only choice left.

Six

The Darkening Heart

The first signs were subtle.

At first, Thorne had only felt a slight weakness in his chest, a tightness that made it difficult to breathe. It was nothing more than a fleeting discomfort—an ache in his body that he could ignore. But over the days, it grew worse. His body felt heavier, like the weight of the curse was settling into his bones, pulling him deeper into its grip. His usually sharp eyes were clouded, his movements slower, his strength ebbing away as though it were being siphoned by an unseen force.

Liora could see the change in him before he even spoke of it. The pallor of his skin was unnatural, and the once-proud posture that defined him as a prince seemed to wither beneath the weight of something darker than any physical ailment. The curse was spreading through him, slowly and insidiously, its tendrils weaving their way into the very marrow of his bones.

It was as though it had begun to feast on his vitality, devouring him piece by piece.

He tried to mask it. He tried to hide it from her, as he always had, but Liora could see the subtle tremors in his hands when he reached for something, the labored breath that escaped him when he thought she wasn't looking. And though he never admitted it, she knew the truth. She knew the curse was claiming him.

Every night, she would lie awake beside him, listening to the sound of his breathing as it grew more labored, his chest rising and falling with a rhythm that seemed unnatural. She would reach out, brushing her fingers across his brow, feeling the heat that radiated from him. He burned with fever, but it wasn't just the fever that worried her. It was the coldness in his eyes, the distance that had grown between them, as though the very essence of the curse was driving them apart.

And then, the visions began.

At first, they were only fleeting images—snippets of nightmares that Liora could barely recall when she woke. But they grew more vivid with each passing night, and soon they began to feel like warnings. The visions were violent, brutal, and every single one of them was centered on Thorne's death. She would see him in her mind's eye, lying motionless in her arms, blood staining his clothes, his body growing cold. She would hear the sound of his breath—slow, labored, as though he were drowning—and see the panic in his eyes as he reached for her, trying to speak, but unable to.

Each vision was worse than the last.

One night, as the moon hung low in the sky, a new vision tore through her. She saw Thorne standing alone in the middle of a battlefield, surrounded by shadows that seemed to close in around him. His sword was drawn, but he was weary, stumbling, his strength failing. She could feel his desperation, the way his body was betraying him, and then, in the distance, she saw the glint of steel. A figure emerged from the darkness—tall, imposing, and as it approached, she saw the face of the one who would strike him down. It was a stranger, a man she didn't know, but his eyes were cold, filled with malice. And before she could scream, before she could reach him, she saw the blade sink deep into Thorne's side.

The vision was so vivid that she could almost feel the blood on her own hands, could hear the sound of the steel piercing his flesh. She woke with a jolt, gasping for air, her heart pounding in her chest. She looked over at Thorne, lying beside her, his chest rising and falling in the quiet darkness, but her mind was screaming, warning her of the impending doom.

She had tried to tell him, tried to explain the images, the visions that haunted her, but every time she did, he brushed it off, insisting that it was nothing more than the weight of the curse twisting her mind. But Liora knew better. The curse was not just a threat to their hearts—it was a force that would eventually destroy them both.

Days passed, and the visions grew more frequent, more terrifying. Liora could no longer separate reality from the nightmares. Every time she closed her eyes, she saw Thorne dying—whether it was on the battlefield, in their bed, or in the quiet corners of their home. The truth was undeniable. She could see it now, clear as day. The curse was not just a curse of love—it was a curse of death. And there was no escaping it.

As the curse tightened its grip, the tension between them began to build. Thorne grew more distant, though he tried to hide it. He would retreat into himself, spending hours alone in the castle's training yard, his sword slicing through the air with a precision that belied the weakness that had settled in his body. He pushed himself harder, as if willing his body to fight off the poison that was slowly draining him of life.

But Liora could feel it. The distance between them wasn't just physical—it was emotional. The love that had once blossomed so easily between them now felt like a fragile thing, held together by threads that threatened to snap with every passing day. She didn't know how to fix it. She didn't know how to protect him, how to save them both from the curse that was dragging them toward an inevitable end.

And then, one evening, it happened.

They were in the castle's garden, surrounded by the scent of wildflowers and the soft rustling of the trees. Thorne had insisted they walk together, and though Liora could sense the fatigue in his every step, she complied. She had always loved these moments, the quiet serenity of the garden, the feeling of being together with him without the weight of the world pressing on their shoulders.

But tonight, there was no peace to be found.

As they walked, Liora noticed a subtle change in Thorne. His breathing had become shallow, ragged, and his steps faltered, as if his legs could no longer carry his weight. His hand, once strong and sure, was now limp at his side. She could feel the strain in his body, the way he was fighting against the inevitable collapse.

"Thorne, you need to rest," Liora said softly, reaching for his arm to steady him. "You're not well. Please, let me help you."

He shook his head, his face grim. "I'm fine," he lied, though his voice cracked. "I'm not… I'm not weak."

But Liora could see it now—the toll the curse was taking on

him. The slow, painful unraveling of everything that had once been so strong. She didn't need him to say it aloud. She could feel it in her bones, in her heart. *He was dying.*

"Thorne, please," she whispered again, her voice breaking. "You're not fine. I can feel it. I can see it."

His gaze softened as he looked at her, his eyes dark and full of sorrow. He reached out to touch her cheek, his fingers trembling as they brushed against her skin. "Liora, I—"

Before he could finish, Liora felt a sharp pain shoot through her chest, as though the thorns in her hands had pierced her heart. She gasped, stumbling back, her breath coming in ragged gasps. The vision came upon her suddenly, crashing over her like a wave.

She saw Thorne again. This time, he was lying on the cold stone floor, his body pale and still. His hand reached out toward her, but there was no warmth in it—only the cold emptiness of death. His lips moved, but no sound came. She could see the blood staining his clothes, the life draining from him, and for a moment, she thought she might be lost in it forever.

She screamed, but the sound was trapped in her throat, as though the very essence of the curse had stolen her voice.

"Thorne!" she cried out, snapping back to reality. She stumbled forward, her hands reaching for him, but as she did, she saw the fear in his eyes, the realization that the curse had claimed him. That it was too late.

The pain in her chest was unbearable, but it was nothing compared to the pain in her heart. The realization hit her like a ton of bricks. She could not save him. Not this time.

She fell to her knees, clutching her chest as the tears spilled down her face. "No," she whispered, the word escaping her lips in a broken sob. "Please, no."

Thorne dropped to his knees beside her, his hand shaking as he cupped her face. "Liora, don't… don't do this," he pleaded, his voice hoarse. "Please don't give up on me."

She looked at him through tear-filled eyes, and for the first time, she realized just how much she had been holding back. How much she had been trying to protect him, to shield him from the truth. But now, in this moment, she knew there was no escaping it. The curse had already chosen its path. It had already begun to claim them both.

"I love you," she whispered, her voice broken. "But I can't lose you. Not like this."

Thorne's eyes darkened with understanding, the weight of her words sinking deep into his soul. "Then we fight, Liora. We fight for each other."

But even as he said the words, she knew. They couldn't fight forever. The curse was too powerful. The love between them was both their salvation and their destruction. And no matter what they did, it would only be a matter of time before the darkness claimed them both.

Her heart broke as she whispered her final vow, the one thing she knew she could still do for him.

"I'll protect you," she promised, her voice trembling. "No matter the cost."

But deep down, she knew she was lying. She was fighting a battle she couldn't win. And the cost would be more than either of them could bear.

The night pressed down on them like a heavy cloak, and the weight of their shared grief seemed to grow with every passing moment. Thorne's hand trembled as he cupped Liora's face, his thumb brushing away the tears that had stained her cheeks. His breath came in ragged gasps, his chest rising and falling as though the very air was growing thicker, more suffocating.

"Liora," he whispered, his voice a low rasp, full of pain and helplessness. "Please, you can't give up. Not like this. We can fight it—*together*."

Liora's heart twisted in her chest as she looked into his eyes, but the ache inside her, the weight of the curse that had already woven itself into the very fabric of their being, told her that it was futile. No matter how much they wanted to fight it, no matter how much love there was between them, the curse would *not* let them be. It had already begun to tear them apart, and no magic, no will, no desire to be together would change that fact.

She could feel the thorns in her palms, the sharp, biting reminder of the curse that had taken root deep inside her. They were not just a symbol of their bond—they were the physical manifestation of everything that had been set in motion from the moment they met. She had known this would happen, known that the curse would eventually break them. But now that it was so close, now that the end was drawing near, the realization hit her harder than she had ever expected.

"I *won't* let you go," Thorne repeated, his voice a growl, as though each word was a vow made through gritted teeth. His hand tightened around hers, the warmth of his touch a faint reminder of the man she had fallen in love with, the man she had wanted to protect above all else.

Liora shook her head slowly, her vision blurry with tears. "Thorne, you have to let me go. This curse—it will destroy us both. We can't keep pretending that everything will be fine. This… *this* is how it ends."

Thorne's face twisted in anguish. "I won't accept that! I won't lose you, Liora. I can't—*I can't breathe without you.*"

His voice cracked with the admission, and it tore at Liora's soul. Every fiber of her being screamed in protest at the thought of losing him, but she also knew that his suffering was becoming unbearable. He was fading before her eyes—his body weakening, his spirit dimming with every breath.

She closed her eyes, the sharp sting of the thorns in her hands seeming to match the ache in her heart. The visions, the endless, violent images of Thorne's death, played in her mind again—flickering like a reel of film she could not turn off. Every vision was a nightmare of blood, of broken bodies, of loss. She could see the end coming for him, and there was nothing she could do to stop it.

"Thorne," she whispered, her voice barely audible as she let her forehead rest against his. "I love you. I always have. But I can't watch you die because of me. I can't bear to see you suffer like this."

She felt the tremor in his hands as he cupped her face, his eyes wild with panic. "Liora, please, don't say that. Don't *ever* say that. I will never let you go. You are my heart, my soul. Without you—"

His words faltered, as though even saying them made the weight of the truth unbearable. His chest heaved, and Liora could feel his pulse pounding beneath her hands as she gently rested them on his chest. The connection between them was undeniable. She could feel the magic humming beneath her skin, the pulse of their bond—a force of nature that neither of them could control.

But at what cost?

The answer loomed over her, dark and inevitable. They

could not escape it.

She leaned into him, pressing her face to his chest, letting the warmth of his body envelop her for one final moment. She could feel the weight of the curse tightening around them both, squeezing the very breath from her lungs. She knew what she had to do, but the thought of it—of letting him go—ripped her heart out in ways she had never imagined.

She pulled away from him slightly, her gaze unwavering as she looked up into his eyes. Her voice was steady, but the depth of sorrow in her words was undeniable. "I will protect you, Thorne. But in order to save you… I have to let you go. I can't let this curse destroy both of us. You deserve more than this pain."

Thorne's face contorted in a way that made her chest tighten, his eyes flickering with the pain of knowing that she was slipping away from him. "No… please," he begged, his voice breaking. "Liora, I can't—*I can't live without you*. Please don't make me live a life where you're not there."

Liora shook her head, her tears falling freely now as her heart shattered in the quiet of the night. "I will always be with you, Thorne. In your heart, in your memories. I'll be there. But the curse has already claimed us, and I can't bear to watch you suffer any longer."

The last words were the hardest to say. Each syllable felt like a betrayal, each breath an agony that threatened to consume her. The love between them had been a shining light, a hope that had kept them going through the darkness. But the weight of the curse, the certainty of the end, had pulled them into a void from which there was no escape.

Thorne stepped back from her, his hand falling limply at his side as he stared at her, his face pale with shock. "You… You're saying you'll *leave* me?"

"I have to," Liora whispered, her heart breaking with every word. "This is the only way."

Thorne shook his head violently, his breath ragged. "No… No, you *can't* leave me, Liora. I love you. I would rather die than live without you."

And that was the truth, wasn't it? He would die, she knew. His body was already breaking beneath the strain of the curse. Every second he spent tethered to her, to the bond that had been forged in pain and magic, brought him closer to his own destruction. The darkness was taking him.

But so was she.

The two of them were trapped in an endless spiral, a dance between love and death, between salvation and damnation. And no matter how much she wanted to fight against it, no matter how much she wanted to tear herself away from this curse that had already taken root, the truth remained: there was no escaping it.

Liora reached for his hand, her fingers trembling as she clasped his. The thorns in her palms seemed to writhe in response, as though the magic had sensed the shift between them. The moment she touched him, the power between them surged like a storm unleashed, wild and uncontrolled. It filled the air around them, swirling in the space between them, and Liora could feel it pulling at her very soul.

Thorne's grip tightened on her hand, his eyes desperate. "I *can't* lose you," he whispered, his voice breaking under the weight of the plea. "Please… let me save you."

"Let me save you instead," she breathed, her voice filled with finality, though it broke her heart to speak the words.

The space between them hummed with the intensity of their

love, the curse, and the impending finality of their bond. Liora closed her eyes for just a moment, feeling the steady rhythm of his heart beneath her hand, the pulse of their connection, and the weight of their fate.

"I will always love you," she whispered. "Always."

And in that instant, as the air around them shimmered with the weight of the magic that bound them, Liora knew that the choice had already been made. The curse would have its toll, no matter what they did. But at least she could give him something—one last piece of peace before the end came.

Before it all ended.

And in that moment, as the darkness crept in on them both, the curse finally settled into her heart, a final, bitter truth. The bond between them was too strong to break. And love… love would be the thing that killed them both.

Seven

The Heart's Echo

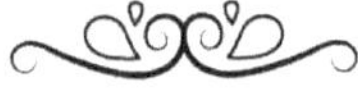

The night hung heavy with a cold, biting air, the moon barely visible behind a blanket of clouds. Liora stood at the window of their modest refuge, gazing out into the dark expanse of the wilderness. The trees swayed in the wind, their branches creaking like old bones, casting long shadows that seemed to reach toward her, grasping at the edge of the world. Somewhere in the distance, an owl called, its eerie cry cutting through the silence.

Inside, Thorne lay in a state of restless sleep, his face pale and drawn, his chest rising and falling with labored breaths. Liora could hear the faint, rhythmic thud of his heart, weaker with each passing day. The curse had taken hold of him, its grip tightening until he seemed little more than a shadow of the man he once was.

She wanted to be strong for him, wanted to believe that they could overcome it—that there was still hope. But the longer they remained in hiding, the more her doubts grew. The visions of Thorne's death were no longer fleeting—they were constant, filling her dreams, haunting every waking moment. She could feel the weight of the future pressing down on her, a future that seemed inevitable, one where the curse would consume them both.

But tonight, something was different. The air felt heavier, charged with a tension that Liora couldn't explain. It was as if the world itself was holding its breath, waiting for something to happen.

A knock at the door broke her thoughts.

Liora's heart skipped a beat, her breath catching in her throat. She quickly moved toward the door, her pulse quickening. She wasn't expecting anyone—not here, in the wilderness, so far from the kingdom. But as she reached for the handle, she hesitated. Something in her gut twisted with unease. She couldn't shake the feeling that this was not a visit from an ally.

She slowly opened the door.

Sorin stood there, his face shadowed in the dim light of the flickering candle behind her. His eyes met hers, but there was something cold in his gaze—something unfamiliar. Sorin had always been her closest friend, the one she trusted above all others. He had been there for her when no one else had, guiding her through the darkest times. But now, as she looked at him, she wondered if she had truly known him at all.

"Sorin?" she asked, her voice betraying the uncertainty she felt. "What are you doing here?"

His lips curled into a faint, cold smile. "You thought you could hide forever, Liora? You thought you could escape the inevitable?" His words were laced with something sharp, something that sent a chill running down her spine.

Liora's heart stilled. There was something wrong—so very wrong—about the way he spoke. The man she had once trusted had changed, and she could feel the weight of his betrayal hanging in the air like a storm ready to break.

"You need to leave," Sorin said, his tone low and dangerous now, the smile gone. "It's too late for you to resist."

Liora took a step back, her hand instinctively going to the doorframe for support. "What are you talking about? Sorin, what's happening?"

He stepped forward, pushing past her into the room, his movements swift and unsettling. "The curse," he said, his voice suddenly sharp, his eyes gleaming with something dark and malicious. "You don't understand, do you? The curse is not something to be fought—it is something to be embraced. I've made a choice, Liora. And I suggest you make yours quickly."

Liora's stomach dropped. "What do you mean?" she demanded, her voice barely above a whisper. "You've always been with me, Sorin. Always. How could you—"

Sorin turned sharply to face her, his gaze darkening. "I've been with you, yes. But I've always known there was something more at stake here than your little rebellion. The curse is not just a tragedy. It's the key to power—unlimited power. I've made a deal with those who see its true potential. The curse must be fulfilled, Liora. And you, *you* are the key."

Liora's heart raced, and her mind spun in a thousand directions. She couldn't believe what she was hearing. Sorin had betrayed her—betrayed everything they had fought for. The weight of it settled like a stone in her chest.

"I won't let you do this," she said, her voice trembling with fury. "I won't let you use me to fulfill this curse."

Sorin's smile returned, but it was cold—insincere. "You

don't have a choice. None of us do. The curse is bigger than you, bigger than me, bigger than anything you could ever understand. I've aligned myself with those who see it for what it truly is. And I will use you to make sure it's fulfilled. If you fight me, you'll only bring destruction to yourself. But if you cooperate, you'll be part of something far greater than anything you could ever imagine."

Liora recoiled, disgust swirling inside her. "You're a fool," she spat, her voice filled with a fury that burned deep in her chest. "You don't see what you're doing. You don't understand the cost of this! You're willing to sacrifice everything—everyone—for power?"

Sorin stepped closer, his eyes narrowing as he studied her with an almost predatory gaze. "I see everything, Liora. I see the future. The curse will bring us power beyond measure, and with it, we can reshape the world as we see fit."

The room seemed to close in on her. The weight of his words settled over her like a suffocating fog. Her closest ally, the one she had trusted with her life, was now her enemy. He had chosen the darkness over everything they had fought for, over the love she and Thorne shared.

She backed away slowly, her heart pounding in her chest. "You're not the man I thought you were, Sorin."

Sorin watched her with a detached curiosity, as if her words held no weight. "The curse is already in motion, Liora. It's too late to stop it. You can't fight destiny."

Before she could respond, she heard a weak cough from behind her. Thorne. He had been lying in bed, resting, but his eyes were now open, his gaze fixed on the scene unfolding before him.

Sorin turned to look at him, his expression darkening. "The

prince," he said, almost mockingly. "Still alive, I see. How touching."

Thorne tried to sit up, his hand clutching the side of the bed, but his body betrayed him. He was too weak, his energy drained by the curse. His voice was hoarse when he spoke. "What's going on here, Sorin? What have you done?"

Sorin's smile widened as he turned back to Liora. "I didn't want to involve him, but I suppose it was inevitable. You're both trapped now. The curse is already taking hold of you. Your fate is sealed. You'll either submit to it… or die."

Liora's heart raced as she moved toward Thorne, her hand reaching out to steady him. She could see the fear in his eyes, the realization that they were running out of time. Sorin's betrayal had shifted everything. They couldn't hide anymore. They couldn't run.

"You're wrong," Liora said, her voice cold with determination. "We will fight. We won't let you win."

Sorin's eyes flickered with amusement. "You can fight all you want, Liora. But the curse will win in the end. It always does."

Suddenly, Sorin's demeanor shifted. He turned sharply, and before Liora could react, he raised a hand, a pulse of dark energy crackling around his fingers. The room seemed to grow colder, the air thick with the weight of his magic.

Liora gasped, but it was too late. The force of the magic slammed into her chest, sending her stumbling backward. She crashed into a nearby table, the impact knocking the breath out of her. Thorne cried out, trying to push himself to his feet, but his body betrayed him. He collapsed back onto the bed, his face pale with pain.

"Sorin, stop!" Liora shouted, her heart racing as she pushed herself to her feet. The world around her spun, but she fought to steady herself. The curse's power was already overwhelming her, but she refused to give in. Not yet.

Sorin watched her with amusement, the darkness in his eyes growing deeper. "You think you can stop me?" he taunted. "You are nothing but a pawn in this game, Liora. And when the curse is fulfilled, you will see the truth. We will rise. And all who stand in our way will fall."

Liora's heart pounded as she backed away, her mind racing for a way out. She had no choice but to flee. If Sorin was truly allied with those who sought to use the curse to their advantage, then she and Thorne were in more danger than they had ever imagined.

"Sorin, please," she said, her voice shaking with a mixture of fear and defiance. "You don't have to do this. You don't have to be part of this darkness."

But Sorin's expression remained unchanged. His gaze flickered back to Thorne. "You can save yourself, Liora," he said softly, almost as if pitying her. "But it will cost you. You'll have to choose—choose to leave him behind. Choose to let the curse consume him. Or, together, you'll both fall. It's inevitable."

Liora's heart clenched at his words. She could see the truth of them, feel the weight of his betrayal, and yet, she knew she could never leave Thorne. Not now. Not ever.

As Sorin moved toward the door, Liora stepped forward, her voice steady despite the chaos swirling in her chest. "I won't let you control me. I won't let you destroy what's left of us."

Sorin stopped, glancing back over his shoulder, his eyes gleaming with a cold, sinister light. "We'll see, Liora. We'll see."

And with that, he was gone.

Liora stood there, her breath shallow, her heart pounding in her chest. She could feel the weight of the decision pressing on her. Sorin had betrayed her, yes. But more than that, he had given her no choice. The world had changed. And now, she and Thorne had to face the darkness together.

She rushed to Thorne's side, kneeling beside him as he struggled to sit up. The room was thick with the tension of their situation—of the betrayal that had shattered everything they had once believed. But as their eyes met, as their fingers intertwined, Liora knew one thing: she would never abandon him.

"We need to leave," she said quietly, her voice full of determination. "We need to escape. And we'll find a way to break the curse. Together."

Thorne looked at her, his eyes filled with both fear and love. "We'll fight," he whispered, his voice hoarse but steady. "We'll fight to the end. Together."

And so, with no more words between them, Liora and Thorne fled into the night, away from the castle, away from the betrayal, into a world that was now darker and more dangerous than ever before.

Liora could feel the weight of the night pressing down on her as they fled into the wilderness, the sounds of the forest eerily quiet around them, as if the world itself was holding its breath. The dark trees loomed overhead, their branches casting twisted, gnarled shadows across the ground. The path they had chosen was rugged, the terrain unfamiliar, but it was the only place they could run—*the only place they could hide.*

Thorne's breath was labored beside her, his body struggling to keep up despite his valiant efforts. Every time he stumbled, she was there to catch him, her heart breaking a little more with every passing moment. She could see the toll the curse had taken on him, the way his once-strong frame seemed to wilt under the burden. The power that had once coursed through him like fire was now nothing more than a faint spark, smothered by the curse's insidious grasp.

But it wasn't just the physical toll that wore on them. It was the betrayal that had come from someone they both trusted—Sorin. The one man who had always stood by them, who had pledged his loyalty to her cause, had turned against them without a second thought. The truth of it settled in her chest like a jagged shard of glass, each breath a reminder that she had been fooled. Sorin had chosen power. He had chosen darkness, and with it, he had condemned them all to a future of pain and suffering.

Liora's mind raced with questions she didn't have the answers to. How had Sorin been so easily swayed? What was it that the dark faction promised him in exchange for betraying them? She couldn't stop herself from wondering if they had ever truly known him at all.

And the worst part? The betrayal didn't just come from Sorin. It came from the very curse that had woven its tendrils into their hearts, the thing that had poisoned the man she loved. It was the same curse that now had Thorne in its grip, draining the life from him, twisting him into something he couldn't control.

She glanced at him again, her heart aching as she watched him falter. The pale moonlight illuminated his face, casting harsh shadows that made him look even more fragile than he was. His brow was slick with sweat, his breathing shallow. He was fighting to keep up, to hold on for as long as he could, but she could see the strain in his every movement.

"Thorne," she whispered, stopping in her tracks. She reached for him, gripping his arm to steady him. His head tilted toward her, his eyes unfocused for a moment as if he were trying to clear the fog from his mind.

"I'm okay," he murmured, though his voice lacked conviction. "We just need to keep moving. We can't stop now."

Liora shook her head, her hands trembling as she gently cupped his face. "Thorne, we *can't* keep running. Not like this. You're getting weaker. We need to rest. We need to think."

He opened his mouth to argue, but his words faltered as he swayed slightly on his feet. She could see the exhaustion in his eyes, the resignation that had begun to settle in. And in that moment, Liora knew that if they didn't stop—if they didn't rest—he would collapse, and it might be the end for them both.

"We'll only rest for a moment," she said firmly, though it felt like an eternity. "Just long enough for you to breathe."

Thorne gave her a weak smile, the corners of his lips twitching in an attempt to reassure her. "You always did know how to take charge," he said softly, his voice barely more than a whisper.

Liora swallowed the lump in her throat and led him to a nearby rock, where they both sat, the damp earth beneath them cold and unforgiving. The moonlight filtered through the trees above, casting a soft glow that made the wilderness feel almost serene, but it couldn't drown out the terror that gnawed at her insides.

The silence between them felt heavy, oppressive. Liora couldn't tear her eyes away from Thorne's face. He was slipping further from her, the curse draining him, and with each passing moment, she felt the bond between them grow tighter, suffocating. She could feel the pull of the curse like a tightening noose around her own heart.

"I don't know what to do anymore," she confessed, her voice raw. "I don't know how to save you, Thorne."

His eyes met hers, and for the first time in days, there was a flicker of something—some spark of the man she had once known—behind the fatigue and the pain. His hand reached for hers, his fingers cold and trembling as he gripped her tightly.

"You've done more than enough," he said, his voice steady despite the weakness that clung to him. "We're together, Liora. And that's all that matters. You're the only one who's kept me going. I don't need saving, not from you. Not from this."

The sincerity in his voice made her heart ache even more, a flood of emotion threatening to drown her. She wanted to believe that there was a way out, that they could find a solution, that they could escape the grip of the curse that held them both captive. But the longer they ran, the more she realized that the only way out might be through death—the death of one of them, or the death of the bond that tied them together.

As she sat there, her mind racing, the sound of distant footsteps reached her ears. She stiffened, her hand instinctively moving toward the dagger at her waist, but Thorne grabbed her wrist before she could react.

"Don't," he whispered, his grip gentle but firm. "It's too late for that. We're already past the point of no return."

Liora looked down at him, her heart heavy with grief. He was right. The curse had already claimed them. All they could do now was face it, together.

The footsteps grew louder, and a shadow emerged from the darkness. Liora's hand tightened on the dagger as the figure came into view, but the voice that called her name made her freeze.

"Liora!" Sorin's voice rang out, cutting through the stillness of the night.

Liora's heart skipped in her chest. *Sorin?* She hadn't expected him to follow them—not so soon. Her mind raced with confusion and a sickening sense of betrayal. What was he doing here? What did he want from them now?

He stepped closer, his silhouette emerging from the shadows, his face unreadable. Behind him, a few figures loomed, cloaked in darkness. They were not just here for answers. They were here for *them*.

"Go back, Sorin," Liora said, her voice steady despite the knot of panic that twisted in her stomach. "We don't have time for this. You've made your choice. You betrayed us."

Sorin's eyes glinted with something she couldn't place—something cruel, something she didn't want to understand. "You think you can run forever, Liora?" he asked, his tone mocking. "You think you can escape what's been set in motion? You're both bound to it, whether you like it or not. The curse will claim you. But I'm here to make sure it happens, sooner rather than later."

Liora felt a surge of anger rise within her, but she kept her voice calm. "You don't control me, Sorin. You've made your choice. Now leave us be."

Sorin took a step forward, his eyes narrowing. "You're a fool, Liora. The power the curse offers will give us everything we need. Don't you understand? The gods chose *me*, not you."

Liora's grip tightened on her dagger, the weight of her resolve settling like iron in her chest. "Then you can have the curse," she said, standing tall despite the weakness in her legs. "But we'll never let you win."

Sorin's lips curled into a smile, but there was no joy in it—

only malice. "We'll see how long your fight lasts, Liora. You can't escape what you are."

With a flick of his hand, the figures behind him moved forward, their cloaks billowing in the night air like shadows. Thorne gripped Liora's arm, his eyes pleading.

"Don't fight them, Liora. We can't win this battle."

Liora looked down at him, her heart breaking as she saw the desperation in his eyes. But the fight inside her flared stronger than ever. She could feel the curse pulling at them, dragging them toward an inescapable end. And though it felt like the world was closing in, she couldn't let it happen. Not like this.

"We'll fight, Thorne," she whispered, her voice trembling with determination. "Even if it costs us everything."

And with that, the battle for their future began, the darkness closing in around them like a storm ready to break.

Eight

The Thorn That Binds

The wind howled through the dense forest as Liora and Thorne moved silently beneath the canopy of ancient trees, the darkness of the night creeping along the edges of their path. Each step they took seemed to echo in the stillness, a constant reminder of how far they had come—and how far they still had to go. Their journey had led them to this point, to the ruins of an ancient temple that lay hidden deep in the wilderness, a place shrouded in mystery and danger.

The temple was said to hold the answers they desperately sought, the key to breaking the curse that had bound their fates together. But as they approached the overgrown stone structure, something in the air shifted. The trees around them seemed to close in, their branches twisted and gnarled like skeletal hands reaching for the sky. The night air grew colder, and Liora could feel the weight of something ancient pressing against her chest, suffocating her with its presence.

She glanced at Thorne, who walked beside her, his steps slower than usual, his face pale under the moonlight. The curse had taken more from him with each passing day, and it was becoming harder for him to hide the toll it had taken on his body. His eyes were heavy with fatigue, his once-proud posture now slumped with the burden of the curse he had carried all his life. He tried to hide it, but Liora saw the pain in his every movement, the faint tremor in his hands that he couldn't control.

"I'm fine," Thorne said quietly, catching her gaze. "We're almost there."

Liora didn't respond. She could see the way his chest rose and fell with labored breath, the strain in his every movement. He wasn't fine. And she wasn't sure how much longer he could keep going, not with the curse tightening its grip on him, feeding on the bond between them.

The temple loomed ahead, its crumbling walls barely visible through the dense fog that had begun to creep in. The structure, though ancient, still held a sense of power, its stone walls darkened by the weight of time and decay. A pair of large stone columns framed the entrance, their surfaces etched with intricate symbols and runes that seemed to pulse with an eerie energy.

"This is it," Liora murmured, her heart beating faster as she stepped closer to the threshold. "This is where it all began."

Thorne followed her, his eyes scanning the ruins warily. "Stay close," he said, his voice strained. "There's something about this place… it feels wrong."

Liora didn't argue. She knew exactly what he meant. The air around the temple felt thick, heavy with the weight of its past, and she could sense the dark magic that lingered in every crack of the stone, every whispered gust of wind. The curse, its origins, its consequences—all of it was tied to this place. She could feel it in her bones, like a dark pull tugging at the very heart of her soul.

They stepped inside the temple, and Liora immediately felt the shift in the air. It was as if the very stones themselves had absorbed the ancient magic that had once flowed through them, the power of the sorcery that had created the curse now pulsing through the ruins. The walls were lined with faded murals, depicting scenes of battle and sacrifice, of ancient gods and vengeful sorcerers. The images seemed to come to life in the dim light, their faces twisted in agony, their eyes pleading for release.

Liora's fingers brushed against the cold stone, feeling the magic thrumming beneath the surface, as though the walls themselves were alive, waiting for something. She felt the pull again—stronger now, more urgent, as if the temple was calling to her, beckoning her toward its heart.

"Do you feel it?" she whispered to Thorne, her voice barely audible in the oppressive silence.

Thorne's gaze swept the room, his face etched with both fear and determination. "Yes," he said quietly. "It's like the very air here is alive with power. But it's not the kind of magic we're used to. It feels… wrong."

Liora nodded, her pulse quickening as they moved deeper into the temple. The air seemed to grow colder with each step they took, the shadows in the corners stretching longer, darker. The further they went, the more the weight of the temple pressed down on them, and Liora could feel the curse growing stronger, its presence threatening to consume them both.

At the center of the temple stood an altar, its surface carved with ancient symbols, the stone worn and cracked with age. It was here, she knew, that the heart of the curse had been forged. It was here that the dark sorcerer had bound the fates of her ancestors to the curse, creating a bond that had stretched across generations, until it finally found its way to her and Thorne.

Liora's breath caught in her throat as she approached the altar. There, etched into the stone, were the same symbols that had appeared in her visions—the same markings that had been burned into the thorns in her hands. The connection between them was undeniable. The curse had been set in motion long before they were born, and now, it was reaching its conclusion.

Thorne stepped beside her, his gaze falling on the altar, his face pale. "This is where it started," he said softly. "The sorcerer who cursed my family… he must have used this altar to bind us to the curse. To punish us."

Liora nodded slowly, her heart heavy with the weight of what they were about to uncover. "But why us, Thorne? Why are we the ones who have to carry this curse? What did our ancestors do to deserve this?"

Thorne was silent for a long moment, his brow furrowing as he studied the symbols on the altar. "I don't know," he said finally. "But whatever it was, it must have been terrible. And the sorcerer who cursed us… he wanted to make sure no one ever forgot what we had done."

Liora's fingers traced the symbols on the altar, and as she did, she felt a jolt of energy rush through her, her body trembling with the surge of magic. It was the same magic that had been with her since the beginning—since the first time she had felt the thorns in her hands, since the first time she had met Thorne. The bond between them was still strong, still pulsing with life, and Liora could feel it now, deeper than ever before.

Suddenly, a voice echoed through the temple, cutting through the silence with its chilling resonance.

"You've come to learn the truth," the voice said, its tone cold and hollow. "But you will not like what you find."

Liora spun around, her heart racing. She couldn't see anyone, but the voice seemed to come from everywhere at once, reverberating through the walls of the temple.

"Who's there?" she demanded, her voice steady despite the fear rising within her. "Show yourself!"

From the shadows at the far end of the temple, a figure stepped forward—tall and cloaked in darkness. His face was hidden beneath a hood, his features obscured by shadows, but the presence of his magic was undeniable. Liora felt the weight of it pressing down on her, the power radiating from him like a wave crashing against the shore.

"I am the one who cursed your bloodline," the figure said, his voice chilling in its finality. "I am the one who bound you to this fate. And now, you come to me, asking for answers. But the answers you seek will only lead to your destruction."

Thorne's hand instinctively went to the hilt of his sword, but the figure raised a hand, and the air grew colder still. The shadows around them deepened, the temple seeming to close in on them.

"You can't escape," the figure continued, his voice growing darker, more insistent. "The curse has already been fulfilled. The bond is already sealed. And you, Liora, you are the key to its completion."

Liora stepped forward, her heart racing in her chest. "What do you want from us?" she demanded, her voice trembling with a mixture of fear and anger. "Why are we the ones who have to suffer for this?"

The figure's hooded head tilted slightly, as if considering her question. "Your bloodline carries the stain of an ancient wrong. And that stain cannot be cleansed. The curse was created to punish your ancestors, to make sure their legacy would never be forgotten. And now, you and Thorne—your love, your connection—it is the final piece that will complete the cycle."

Liora's mind spun with confusion and dread. "No," she whispered, shaking her head. "We don't deserve this. We didn't do anything wrong. You can't make us pay for something that happened so long ago."

The figure's cold laugh echoed through the temple, reverberating off the walls. "You are the descendants of the guilty, Liora. You cannot escape what has been done. The curse is yours to bear. And when it is completed, you will both die, and your bloodline will finally be erased."

Liora stumbled back, her breath catching in her throat. She could feel the bond between her and Thorne, the magic that pulsed through them both, growing stronger by the second. The weight of the figure's words pressed down on her, suffocating her with the knowledge that their love, their connection, was the key to their destruction.

"No," Thorne said, his voice hoarse, filled with defiance. "We will not let you win. We will fight this curse, even if it costs us everything."

The figure's eyes glowed with an eerie light beneath the hood, and he raised his hands, his magic crackling through the air. "You cannot fight destiny, Thorne Halloway. It was *made* for you. It was *designed* for you. And now, you must accept it."

The ground beneath them trembled, and the temple seemed

to come alive with the

weight of ancient magic. Liora reached for Thorne's hand, gripping it tightly as the darkness closed in around them. They had come seeking answers.

But all they had found was their doom.

The air in the temple seemed to crackle, as if it too was aware of the looming tension between them and the figure cloaked in darkness. Liora could feel the weight of the magic growing stronger with each heartbeat, each breath. It was as if the very walls of the temple were closing in, pressing down on her, forcing her to accept a fate she could not control. Her fingers tightened around Thorne's hand, her heart racing as the figure before them shifted, his presence growing more oppressive, more powerful.

"Thorne, we can't do this alone," Liora whispered, her voice strained. "We need to figure out a way to break this curse—together."

Thorne's grip tightened in return, his face pale but his eyes burning with a quiet fury. "We won't let him control us," he said, his voice low and filled with determination. "I won't let this curse take you from me. Not now. Not ever."

The figure in the shadows laughed, a low, chilling sound that sent a shiver down Liora's spine. "You still don't understand, do you?" His voice echoed around them, growing louder, more commanding. "The curse cannot be broken by love. It was never meant to be broken. It is not something that can be fought. It is a force that will consume you both."

Liora's breath caught as his words sank in. "Consume us? But how?" she asked, her voice shaking. "You said the curse was created to punish Thorne's ancestors. Why are we still being punished? Why *now*?"

The figure's gaze turned cold, and for the first time, Liora saw a flicker of something ancient and terrible in the depths of his eyes. "The curse was created not only for punishment. It was created as a binding force—meant to tie your bloodline to the very core of death itself. The sorcerer who cursed your ancestors was no mere man. He was a master of dark magic, and he used his power to make sure that the Halloway name would never escape the weight of that darkness."

Liora's mind raced, the pieces of the puzzle beginning to fall into place. "So it was never about love," she said, her voice barely a whisper. "It was about control. The curse binds us, forces us together... *but it also kills us.*"

"Yes," the figure said, his voice dripping with satisfaction. "The curse was never about love between you two. It was always about destruction. About the inevitable end that your bloodline was always destined to face."

Thorne stepped forward, his eyes flashing with anger. "I won't let you control us," he said, his voice shaking with rage. "We will find a way to break this. We will stop you."

The figure's gaze narrowed. "You think you can fight it? You think you can defy destiny? You have always been weak, Thorne Halloway. Always bound to the sins of your ancestors, always shackled by the curse that courses through your veins. Your love for Liora will be the very thing that brings you down."

Liora's heart pounded in her chest, her breath coming in shallow gasps as she felt the magic around them shift. The curse—it was not just a force that had been placed on them. It was a living, breathing thing, wrapped tightly around their hearts, consuming them from the inside out. She could feel the weight of it growing stronger, pressing against her chest like an iron weight.

"We will *not* let this happen," Liora said, her voice filled with determination. "We will fight. We will find a way to *end* this curse, even if it means sacrificing everything."

The figure's laughter grew louder, filling the space around them until it seemed to vibrate through the walls of the temple. "You believe you have the power to break it? You believe that your love for each other is enough? You're wrong. You're all wrong."

Liora felt the air around her grow thick with the dark energy that the figure was wielding. The temperature in the room dropped, and she could see the faint breath in front of her face, the chill creeping through her bones. She turned to Thorne, her heart breaking as she saw the pain in his eyes—the strain of the curse, the weight of what they were facing.

"We have to act now, Thorne," she said, her voice trembling with urgency. "This is our only chance."

Thorne's hand gripped hers tighter, his resolve clear despite the weariness in his eyes. "We will make it through this, Liora. We have to. I'll fight for you. I'll fight for us."

She looked at him, her heart swelling with love and terror. How much longer could they run? How long could they fight against something that was stronger than them both? The curse was inside them, wrapped around their hearts, pulling them toward an inevitable end. But even so, she refused to give up. She would not let the darkness win. Not without a fight.

As if reading her thoughts, the figure's voice echoed through the room, its coldness wrapping around her like a vice. "It's already too late. You are already bound. The bond between you both is irreversible. The moment you embraced each other, the curse was sealed. There is no escaping it now."

Liora's breath hitched. The figure's words were like a punch to the gut. The bond between them—the curse—they had both known that it was growing stronger, that it was consuming them. But hearing it spoken aloud—knowing that their fate was sealed, that there was no way out—was more than she could bear.

"No…" Liora whispered, shaking her head in disbelief. "There has to be a way. There must be something—*anything* we can do."

The figure's cold, dead eyes watched her with a sense of finality, as though he had already won. "There is only one way," he said. "The bond can be severed, but only through the ultimate sacrifice. Only one of you can live. And the other must die."

Liora's chest tightened, her heart threatening to burst from her chest. Thorne stepped forward, his jaw set in a hard line. "We will never let that happen. We will fight. We'll find a way. We'll break the curse. You *can't* make us choose."

The figure's smile was cruel, twisted with the knowledge of his own power. "It is not a choice," he said softly, his voice cold as ice. "It is a law of magic. And it is a law you will both learn the hard way."

As he finished speaking, the ground beneath them trembled, a deep, resonating hum that vibrated through the stone walls. The room seemed to warp, the shadows stretching unnaturally, reaching for them as if the temple itself were alive, its very essence bound to the curse. The air grew thick, suffocating, and Liora could feel the weight of the curse pressing on her chest, threatening to crush her.

Thorne reached for her, his hand clasping hers tightly. His

body was weak, his strength draining with each passing second, but his resolve was unwavering.

"I won't let you die, Liora," he said, his voice fierce, desperate. "I won't let this curse take us. We'll fight it. We have to."

Liora looked into his eyes, her heart shattering as she saw the love and fear there, the strength and the weakness. The curse had torn them apart in ways they could not understand, but their love was still alive, still burning within them. And in that moment, she realized that no matter what happened, she would never let go of him.

"Thorne," she whispered, her voice trembling with emotion. "I love you."

The words hung in the air between them like a promise—a vow that no curse could break. They had come so far, fought so hard, and yet the end was closing in on them. But Liora refused to give in to the darkness. Not without a fight.

The figure watched them with a cold, calculating gaze. "Your love is the very thing that will destroy you both. And there is nothing you can do to change it."

A wave of dark energy surged forward, and Liora felt herself being pulled into its grip, the curse tightening its hold on her, threatening to swallow her whole. The room seemed to spin, the shadows closing in around them.

But even as the darkness pressed in, even as the curse began to claim them both, Liora and Thorne clung to each other, their hearts beating in time with the magic that bound them.

There was no escape.

There was only the choice.

And in that choice, they would find out just how much they were willing to sacrifice for love.

Nine

The Breaking Point

The air was thick with tension as Liora stumbled through the dense forest, her breath ragged, her heart pounding painfully in her chest. Each step sent a jolt of agony through her, and she could feel the thorns buried deep within her skin twisting, growing, as if the very essence of the curse was clawing its way into her heart. The pain was unbearable, a constant, unrelenting pressure that crushed her from the inside out. Every breath she took felt like it might be her last.

Beside her, Thorne moved with a grim determination, his face pale, his eyes shadowed with worry. His once-proud stature had shrunk with the weight of the curse, and the love they shared had become both a blessing and a curse. As much as they fought to break free of its hold, it seemed to grow stronger every day, tightening its grip on them both.

Liora had felt it from the very beginning—the moment their

hearts had first intertwined, the instant they had truly touched, they had been marked. But now, as the thorns in her chest twisted painfully, the truth was undeniable. The curse was no longer just a force they could ignore. It was a part of them—an inescapable, suffocating presence that had taken root deep inside their souls.

"Liora," Thorne said, his voice rough, strained. He stopped in his tracks and turned to face her, his hand reaching out, but she could see the hesitation in his eyes. His breath came in shallow gasps, his body trembling with the strain of carrying the weight of the curse for so long.

"Thorne, we can't keep running," she whispered, her voice barely audible over the sharp wind that howled through the trees. She felt the crushing weight of her own words, the inevitability of their situation pressing down on her like a vice. "We have to end this. We have to face the curse before it destroys us both."

Thorne's face twisted with a mixture of pain and determination. "I know," he said, his voice hoarse, his hand tightening on hers. "But it's too late, Liora. The curse is too strong. The thorns in you—they're killing you. I can feel it. Every second I stay near you, I'm losing you."

Liora closed her eyes, a sharp wave of pain slicing through her chest as the thorns deepened their grip. She clutched her heart, feeling the dark energy pulsing beneath her skin. The curse was taking everything from her, and she could feel herself slipping away, piece by piece. The pain in her chest was the least of her worries now. It was the way it threatened to consume her entirely—the way it felt like the life was draining from her with every beat of her heart.

She shook her head, forcing her eyes open to meet his. "You

can't do this, Thorne. You can't give up on me now." Her voice wavered, and she reached for him, her fingers brushing against his trembling skin. "Please, don't sacrifice yourself. I won't let you."

His gaze hardened, his jaw clenching as though the very idea of losing her was tearing him apart. "Liora, I love you. I always have. But I can't watch you die because of me." His voice cracked, a faint tremor of anguish running through his words. "I can't lose you, not like this."

She took a step back, her heart pounding as she felt the pull of the curse tightening around her. Every breath she took, every thought that passed through her mind, was overshadowed by the suffocating weight of it. The bond they shared, the love they had nurtured—it was killing them. Slowly, methodically, it was killing them both.

"I won't let you do this, Thorne," Liora said fiercely, her voice breaking with the weight of her emotions. She stepped closer to him, her hand reaching for his, her grip firm despite the trembling in her limbs. "We will find another way. There has to be a way to break this curse. We can't give up on each other."

Thorne's eyes softened for a moment, and Liora saw the love he had always carried for her, the depth of his soul, reflected in his gaze. But that love was tainted now. It was twisted, corrupted by the curse. She could feel it in every fiber of her being—the way the bond between them was now a curse, not a blessing.

"I've seen the way you suffer, Liora," Thorne said, his voice low and filled with regret. "And I can't bear it. If the only way to save you—to save *us*—is to sever this bond, then I'll do it. I'll make the sacrifice, even if it means I have to die."

Liora's heart shattered at his words, her chest tightening as if the thorns were now strangling her very soul. "No, Thorne," she pleaded, her voice rising in desperation. "You can't! I won't lose you! I won't let you do this! There has to be another way!"

Thorne's face was contorted with grief, his body trembling with the weight of the decision he was about to make. He reached out, his hands gentle as they cupped her face, his thumb brushing away the tears that had begun to fall. "Liora," he whispered, his voice breaking. "I can't live with the thought of losing you, but I can't live with the thought of killing you either. I'll do whatever it takes to protect you."

Liora shook her head, her heart breaking with each passing moment. "Please," she whispered, her voice barely more than a breath. "I won't survive without you."

The wind howled around them, the forest around them eerily still as the bond between them seemed to pulse, the magic in the air growing heavier, darker. Liora could feel the pull of the curse more strongly than ever before, the energy that coursed through her veins making her heart ache with its intensity. It was suffocating, consuming, and she could feel the end drawing closer with every passing second.

Thorne stepped back, his expression hardening with the weight of his decision. "I have to do this, Liora. For you. For us."

The words cut through her like a blade. Her breath hitched, her chest tightening with fear, with love, with an anguish that threatened to consume her. She couldn't—*she wouldn't*—let him sacrifice himself. Not after everything they had been through. Not after everything they had shared.

She reached for him, her hand trembling as it found his, and she pulled him toward her, forcing him to look at her, to *see* her.

"I will not let you go," Liora said, her voice filled with raw emotion. "I refuse to lose you. I love you, Thorne. I would rather die than live without you. But I *will not* let you die for me. Not like this. Not now."

Thorne's eyes softened, his gaze filled with the same desperation, the same love that burned within her. For a moment, the world around them seemed to fall away—the curse, the bond, the endless darkness—they were nothing in the face of the love that connected them. The very force that had threatened to destroy them was also the force that had brought them together. And for that, they would fight.

Liora's heart beat in time with his, the magic between them flaring, pulsing like a wildfire. She felt it—the surge of energy that coursed through her, through *them*. It was the same power that had bound them together, that had marked them from the very start. It was both their salvation and their doom.

"Thorne," she whispered, her voice trembling with the force of her love. "I won't let you make this decision alone. If we're going to face this curse, we do it together. No more sacrifices. We'll fight it. Together."

Thorne's hand tightened around hers, and for the first time in what felt like an eternity, Liora saw the strength returning to his eyes. He was still weak, still fading under the weight of the curse, but there was something more now—something that burned brighter than the darkness closing in around them.

"We face this curse together," Thorne said, his voice steady now, filled with resolve. "Whatever happens, we do it side by side."

And in that moment, with the thorns in her chest aching, threatening to consume her whole, Liora knew. She knew that no matter the cost, no matter the consequences, they would face the curse together. The bond that had once been their doom would now be their strength. They would fight for their love, for their future, no matter the cost.

Liora closed her eyes, pressing her forehead to Thorne's, and for the first time in what felt like forever, the world around them seemed to pause. The magic, the curse, the pain—all of it faded as she held onto him, as they held onto each other.

They had made their choice.

And together, they would face whatever came next, no matter the cost.

The night seemed to stretch around them like an endless void, swallowing up everything but the steady rhythm of their breathing. The wind had died down, leaving only the echo of their hearts, beating in synchrony—a fragile thread of connection between two souls bound by fate, love, and a curse that sought to tear them apart.

Liora could feel the thorns in her chest pulsing, a cruel reminder of the bond between them. The pain had become unbearable, a constant throbbing that threatened to take her under. But even as it intensified, she refused to let go. The words they had just spoken—their vow to face the curse together—echoed in her mind. She would not let the darkness take him. Not like this.

She tightened her grip on Thorne's hand, feeling the faint tremor in his fingers. His body was still weakening, his strength ebbing away with every passing moment. She could feel it—the curse was draining him, stealing his life from him. It was almost as though the very air they breathed was poisoned, tainted by the power that sought to consume them both.

But she wouldn't let it. She couldn't.

"Thorne," she whispered, her voice shaky, but filled with determination. She lifted her head to meet his gaze, her heart breaking as she saw the weight of his love and his fear reflected in his eyes. "We have to do this now. We have to find a way to stop it, before it takes us."

Thorne's expression softened, and for a moment, the pain in his eyes was replaced by something else—something fierce, something resolute. "I won't let it take you, Liora," he said, his voice steady, though it trembled with the effort. "Not while I'm still breathing."

Her chest tightened at his words. She could feel the magic swirling around them, the power that had always existed between them, now flaring in a way she had never experienced. The bond that had always pulled them together was now growing, expanding, and she could feel it deep in her very soul.

"I don't want to lose you," she said, her voice breaking as she fought to keep the tears at bay. "But I won't let you sacrifice yourself either. If one of us has to die, then it's me. I won't let you be the one to pay the price."

Thorne's eyes widened, and for a moment, the world around them seemed to stop. The wind, the forest, the temple—all of it faded into the background as he looked at her, his face pale but filled with something she couldn't quite place.

"No," he said, his voice low but firm. "You *can't* make that choice for me, Liora. I won't let you carry that burden. I love you too much to let you give up your life."

Liora's throat tightened, and she reached up to touch his face, feeling the warmth of his skin beneath her fingers. His presence—his very being—was all she had left. And yet, the curse was taking him from her, slowly and inexorably.

"We're bound to this, Thorne," she said softly. "And the more we fight it, the more it pulls us in. But I will *not* let you die for me. We have to find another way. Together."

The desperation in her voice seemed to make something stir within him. He closed his eyes for a moment, as though gathering strength from her words. Then, when he spoke again, his voice was filled with a quiet determination.

"If you're going to fight, then we fight together," he said, his voice hoarse but resolute. "We face it, face *everything* together. We're not meant to fight this alone, Liora. We never have been."

She nodded, swallowing the lump in her throat, and in that moment, something shifted between them. It was subtle, a delicate shift in the energy that surrounded them, but Liora could feel it—a growing sense of unity, of purpose, of love that transcended the darkness threatening to tear them apart.

They stood there for a long moment, the air heavy with the weight of their decision. The thorns in Liora's chest pulsed again, and the pain was nearly unbearable, but she refused to let it show. She refused to give in to the curse, to let it control her. She had already given everything to Thorne—her heart, her soul—and she would not let that be destroyed.

But then, as if the universe itself had heard their vow, the ground beneath their feet trembled. A low rumble echoed through the temple, and the shadows in the corners of the room seemed to writhe, as though something were stirring within the very heart of the stone.

Liora gasped, her hand flying to Thorne's arm as the air around them seemed to change, growing thick with magic. The very walls of the temple seemed to pulse with life, the runes etched into the stone glowing faintly, their symbols shifting, moving, as if alive.

"It's happening," Thorne said, his voice thick with realization. He gripped her hand tightly, his other hand reaching for the sword at his side. "The curse is pushing back. It knows we've made our choice."

Liora's heart raced, and she could feel the energy in the room intensifying, crackling around them like a storm about to break. The walls seemed to close in, the air heavy with the ancient magic that had been buried here for centuries.

"We have to stop it," Liora said urgently, her voice filled with determination. "We have to fight back."

But as the words left her lips, the temperature in the room plummeted. The air around them grew thick with darkness, and she could feel the magic in the temple coiling, tightening, ready to strike. The very essence of the curse was being pulled into the space around them, feeding on their emotions, on the love they shared.

And then, from the shadows, a figure emerged.

It was a man, tall and cloaked in darkness, his features obscured by the shadow of his hood. His presence was suffocating, a dark force that seemed to absorb the very light around him. The air seemed to grow colder still, and Liora could feel the energy of the curse swelling, a tangible force that was closing in on them.

"You cannot escape this," the figure said, his voice deep, resonating through the temple as if it were part of the very stone itself. "The bond is complete. There is no way to break it."

Liora's heart skipped a beat. She could feel the power of the figure, the dark magic that emanated from him. This was no ordinary sorcerer—this was the one who had cursed them. The one who had set the chain of events into motion centuries ago.

Thorne stepped in front of her, his sword drawn, his body poised in defense. "We will find a way," he said, his voice unwavering. "We won't let you win."

The figure chuckled, the sound low and chilling. "You have no choice. The curse is yours to bear. You will either die by its hand or be consumed by it. There is no other way."

Liora's chest tightened, and she could feel the thorns in her chest reacting to the figure's presence, the curse pressing against her heart, tightening its grip. It was so much stronger now, pulling at her, as if it wanted to devour her completely. She could feel herself being drawn into it, into the magic that threatened to claim her.

But in that moment, as she looked at Thorne—his face determined, his sword raised in defiance—she realized something. She had never felt more alive than she did in that moment, standing beside him, fighting for everything they had fought for.

"No," she said, her voice steady, filled with a quiet resolve. "We will fight, no matter the cost."

The figure's eyes glinted with amusement as he stepped closer, the shadows seeming to part around him like a shroud. "You can fight all you want," he said, his voice like a low growl. "But you cannot escape the curse. You cannot escape your fate."

Liora stepped forward, her hand gripping Thorne's tightly, her heart racing. She could feel the magic swelling inside her, the bond between them flaring with renewed intensity. The thorns in her chest burned, but she refused to show fear. She had made her choice. They had made their choice. And together, they would face whatever came next.

"You're wrong," Liora said, her voice fierce. "We're not going to let the curse take us. We're going to break it. And we'll do it together."

Thorne turned to her, his face softening with a mixture of love and determination. His grip on her hand tightened, and for the first time in days, she saw a flicker of hope in his eyes.

And together, with the weight of the curse pressing down on them, with the figure looming over them, they stood united. The storm that had raged between them, the pain, the darkness, all of it had brought them to this point. And they would face it. Together.

No matter the cost.

Ten

The Shadowed Heart

The moon hung low in the sky, casting a pale glow over the forest, its light flickering through the trees like a thousand shattered stars. The air was thick with the scent of pine and earth, and yet, something darker seemed to linger—a presence that made Liora's skin crawl, that twisted her insides with a sense of impending doom.

She moved swiftly through the forest, her breath coming in shallow bursts, as though the weight of the night was pressing against her chest. Thorne walked beside her, his steps slow and labored, his once-proud posture now bent with the exhaustion that had taken root in his bones. The curse had drained him to the brink of collapse, but still, he refused to stop, refused to acknowledge how fragile he had become.

Liora glanced at him, her heart tightening in her chest. She couldn't lose him—not now, not when they were so close to finding a way to break the curse that had consumed their lives for so long. She could feel the bond between them—stronger now than it had ever been, pulsing like a living thing, a thread that connected them both, binding them together and pushing them apart all at once.

"Thorne," she said softly, her voice shaking with the weight of everything unsaid between them. "We can't keep going like this. You're getting weaker every day. We need to find a solution, before it's too late."

He glanced at her, his gaze distant, as if he hadn't truly heard her words. "I'll be fine, Liora," he said, though the lie was evident in his tone. "We'll find a way. We always do."

But Liora knew better. She knew the truth in his eyes—the way his strength was fading, the way the curse was slowly breaking him apart from the inside. And she couldn't just stand by and let it happen. She wouldn't.

Ahead of them, the path narrowed, leading into the heart of the forest where the trees grew dense, their trunks twisted like the fingers of ancient gods. A faint light flickered through the shadows ahead, casting eerie shapes on the ground, shapes that seemed to shift and writhe with the wind. As they drew closer, Liora felt a strange pull in her chest—a magnetic force that seemed to call to her, urging her to follow.

"Do you feel that?" she asked, her voice barely above a whisper.

Thorne paused, his brows furrowing as he glanced around. "It's strange," he said, his voice low and guarded. "I feel… something. But it's not the curse. This is different. It's something darker."

They continued forward, the air growing colder with each step, until they reached a clearing in the forest. At its center stood an ancient stone altar, its surface etched with runes that pulsed faintly with an eerie light. The very ground around it seemed to hum with a dark energy that made Liora's stomach twist with unease.

Suddenly, a voice, low and cold, broke the silence.

"You've come to me at last."

Liora's heart skipped a beat as the figure emerged from the shadows, his form tall and imposing, cloaked in darkness. His eyes glowed faintly, an unnatural light that flickered like embers in the night. His skin was pale, almost ghostly, and his features were sharp, like a predator ready to pounce. The air around him seemed to warp, distorting as though the very space between them was bending under the weight of his power.

"Who are you?" Liora demanded, stepping back instinctively, her hand instinctively moving to the dagger at her side.

The figure's lips curled into a smile, his expression cold and calculating. "I am Myrdian," he said, his voice like gravel, harsh and grating. "And I am the one who can destroy the curse that binds you."

Liora's eyes widened, her breath catching in her throat. "You can break it?" she asked, her voice trembling with hope. "How?"

Myrdian took a slow, deliberate step forward, his eyes never leaving hers. "I have the power to destroy the curse," he said, his voice smooth, almost soothing. "But there is a price."

Liora's heart skipped a beat. "What price?"

Myrdian's gaze flickered to Thorne, who had stepped up beside her, his hand gripping the hilt of his sword. The look on his face was one of quiet suspicion, but Liora could feel the flicker of hope in his chest—the same hope that had ignited in her when Myrdian had spoken of destroying the curse.

"The price is simple," Myrdian said, his smile widening. "Liora, you must give yourself to me. Body and soul."

Liora froze, the words hitting her like a blow. She couldn't believe what she was hearing. She shook her head, her thoughts a swirl of confusion and disbelief. "What do you mean?" she demanded, her voice shaking. "I won't give myself to you."

Myrdian's smile remained, but there was no warmth in it. "I've already given you a glimpse of my power," he said. "I am the one who created the curse, the one who bound your ancestors to their fate. And now, I offer you the chance to end it. But it comes at a cost."

Liora stepped back, her mind racing. "You want me to… to *submit* to you? To *join* you in some way?"

"Not just join me," Myrdian said, his voice dark and seductive. "You must give yourself willingly, completely. You must become mine. And in return, I will break the curse. Thorne will live. You will both be free."

Liora's chest tightened, and she felt a sickening knot form in her stomach. She glanced at Thorne, his face pale, his breath shallow. His body was failing, the curse taking him piece by piece, and yet, the thought of surrendering herself to Myrdian, of giving him her soul in exchange for Thorne's life—*it felt wrong*. It felt like a betrayal, not only to herself but to everything she had fought for.

Thorne stepped forward, his voice low and filled with fury. "You're asking her to sacrifice everything—to *sell* herself to you? You think that's worth it?" His eyes locked onto Myrdian's, filled with fire, but also with a hint of desperation. "Liora would never give herself to you, no matter what you offer."

Myrdian's gaze turned cold, his expression unfazed. "I didn't ask for your opinion, Thorne," he said, his voice dripping with venom. "Liora is the key to breaking the curse. And if she doesn't choose to embrace this power, if she doesn't choose to save you, then both of you will perish, bound together by the very curse you seek to escape."

Liora's chest tightened. The words burned through her like acid, the weight of the decision threatening to crush her. She had spent so long fighting for Thorne, for their love, for their future. But now, faced with the impossible choice—surrendering her very soul to save him—she felt as though her world was collapsing around her.

"I can't… I can't do this," she whispered, her voice trembling. "I can't give myself to you, Myrdian. I won't *become* something I'm not. Even if it means losing Thorne."

Myrdian's smile faltered for a brief moment, a flash of something dark and dangerous flickering in his eyes. "You think you have a choice?" he asked, his voice low and dangerous. "You think you can keep running from this? The curse has already claimed you both. The moment you allowed your hearts to intertwine, you sealed your fates."

Liora felt a cold chill wash over her, the weight of his words pressing down on her like a heavy stone. She looked at Thorne again, her heart aching as she saw the struggle in his eyes. He was weak, barely able to stand, but still, he clung to her. He refused to let go. And she could see the terror in his gaze—the fear that he might lose her forever.

"No," Liora said firmly, stepping toward Myrdian, her voice resolute despite the trembling in her chest. "I will never choose this. I will never sacrifice myself for a false promise of freedom."

Myrdian's face twisted with rage. "You are a fool, Liora," he hissed. "The choice has already been made. You just don't see it yet."

Thorne stepped beside her, his voice low but filled with strength. "We will find another way," he said, his grip tightening on the sword at his side. "If you think you can break us with threats, you're mistaken. We won't give in to you."

Myrdian's eyes glowed brighter, his form seeming to shimmer with dark energy as the power around him began to swell. "Then prepare yourselves," he said, his voice rising to a dangerous pitch. "The price for defying me will be greater than you can imagine."

Liora could feel the curse tightening around her heart, the bond between them growing stronger, more painful, more suffocating with every passing moment. She had to make a choice—*but was there even a choice left?*

The darkness swirling around them seemed to close in, the shadows of Myrdian's magic pressing against them like a storm. Every instinct told her to fight, to resist, but in that moment, with the weight of the curse growing stronger, she feared the breaking point was near. Would their love be enough to withstand the pressure?

Would it be enough to save them both?

In the face of impossible choices, Liora knew one thing with certainty. She could not—*would not*—let this curse define them. Not now, not ever.

But the question remained: *How much would she have to sacrifice to protect them both?*

The air in the clearing grew thick with tension, every breath Liora took feeling as though it might be her last. The dark energy swirling around Myrdian pressed in on her chest, suffocating her, threatening to break her resolve. Her heart raced, her mind spinning with thoughts she could not control. The weight of his offer, his demand, hung heavy in the air. To save Thorne, she had to give herself to this dark sorcerer, to give up everything that made her who she was.

Thorne's grip on his sword tightened, and Liora could see the fury and fear in his eyes. He would not let her go. Not without a fight. But they were standing at the edge of a precipice, with no clear way forward. Myrdian's power was immense, and every moment that passed made the curse grow stronger, the thorns in Liora's chest digging deeper.

Myrdian stepped closer, his presence filling the space between them like a suffocating cloud. He tilted his head slightly, his eyes glinting with a cold, calculating light. "You are foolish if you think you have time to resist," he said, his voice low and commanding. "The curse is already upon you both. It will claim you. But there is a way out—for one of you."

Liora shook her head, her hand clutching her chest as the thorns twisted within her, sending fresh waves of pain through her body. The pain was unbearable, but it was nothing compared to the choice Myrdian was forcing upon her. To give herself to him, to surrender her soul, meant the end of everything she had ever known. She would become a vessel for his dark magic, a puppet of his will. And Thorne... he would live, yes, but at what cost? What would he become if she gave herself to this man?

"You're wrong," Liora said, her voice trembling, but fierce. "I won't sacrifice myself for you, not even to save Thorne. You want me to give you my soul, but you have no idea what that would mean. You think you can manipulate me, control me, but I *will not* bow to you."

Myrdian's smile widened, though there was no warmth in

it, just a cold, predatory gleam. "You misunderstand, Liora. I don't need to manipulate you. You're already bound to me. You and Thorne are both tangled in this curse, and the only way to sever it is for you to give yourself freely. Your love, your soul—it is the price that must be paid."

Liora felt the thorns in her chest flare, the pain intensifying, and she gasped, her knees nearly buckling beneath her. She reached out for Thorne, her hand seeking his, and he caught it instantly, pulling her close. His touch was warm, steady, a lifeline in the storm of darkness threatening to drown them both. But his grip on her hand tightened painfully as he too felt the curse wrapping its cold tendrils around him.

"You can't take her," Thorne growled, stepping forward, his face pale but resolute. "I'll never let you control her. Never."

Myrdian looked at Thorne with a mixture of amusement and disdain. "You truly think you can stop me? You, who are already on the brink of death because of the curse? You are weak, Thorne Halloway. This is not a battle you can win."

Thorne raised his sword, his stance unwavering, but Liora could see the strain in his shoulders, the exhaustion in his eyes. The curse was draining him—every moment they spent fighting it, every breath he took, took him one step closer to the edge.

"Thorne, stop!" Liora cried out, her voice cracking. She stepped forward, pulling him back by the arm. "Don't do this. Myrdian's power is beyond us. We can't fight him like this."

Thorne's gaze met hers, and for a moment, the fierce anger in his eyes softened. "I can't just stand by and watch you give yourself to him, Liora. I'll die before I let that happen. I won't lose you."

Liora's chest tightened with the weight of his words, with

the intensity of his love, but she knew. She knew they were running out of time. The curse was too powerful, and every passing moment was pushing them closer to an impossible decision.

She turned back to Myrdian, her voice shaking but determined. "You don't get to make the choice for me," she said, her hands clenched into fists at her sides. "I won't be your sacrifice. You think you can manipulate me with this curse, but I'm not afraid of you."

Myrdian's smile faltered, and the air around him seemed to crackle with dark energy. "You do not understand, Liora. The curse is not just a force of nature—it is a weapon, created by the darkest sorcery. It is bound to your bloodline, to your love for Thorne. And you will both die, slowly, painfully, unless you give me what I want."

Liora's body trembled as she felt the thorns twist deeper within her chest, sending waves of searing pain through her heart. She fell to her knees, her breath coming in gasps, and she saw Thorne's face, twisted with concern, his voice breaking as he reached for her.

"Liora, no!" Thorne cried, dropping to his knees beside her, his hand shaking as he touched her face. "Please, stay with me. I can't lose you."

Liora's heart ached, and the weight of the curse nearly crushed her. The bond between them had always been their strength, but now, it was their greatest weakness. It was pulling them both into the darkness, forcing them to face impossible choices. And yet, as the pain in her chest became unbearable, she knew that she could never—*would never*—let Thorne sacrifice himself.

She reached out, grasping his hand tightly, her voice trembling as she spoke. "Thorne, no matter what happens, I will always love you. I will fight for us. We will find a way."

Myrdian laughed, a deep, menacing sound that echoed through the clearing. "You can fight all you want, but it will change nothing. You are already lost."

Liora could feel his dark energy swirling around them, and she knew the moment had come. The weight of the decision pressed down on her like a stone, suffocating her, threatening to break her.

But she refused. She wouldn't let Myrdian win. She wouldn't let the curse take her, take them both, without a fight.

"I *will* fight you," she whispered, her voice steady despite the pain that threatened to consume her. "We won't surrender. Not to you."

Myrdian's eyes narrowed, and for a moment, his smile faded, replaced by something darker. "Very well," he said softly. "You will see the price of defying me."

The ground beneath them trembled again, the air thickening as the dark magic surged around them, a force of unimaginable power that seemed to warp reality itself. Liora gasped, her body convulsing as the curse pushed against her, trying to take hold of her heart, her soul.

Thorne held her tightly, his voice desperate. "Fight it, Liora! Please, fight it!"

With every ounce of strength she had left, Liora focused on him—on their love, on everything they had been through together. She could feel the bond between them, stronger than it had ever been, pulling her toward him, pulling her away from the darkness that threatened to claim her.

"No matter the cost," she whispered, her voice a vow, a promise. "I won't let you go, Thorne."

With those words, a surge of power erupted from her chest, a pulse of magic that rippled through the temple, sending shockwaves through the air. The thorns in her chest flared, the pain becoming unbearable, but she held on. She clung to him, to the love they shared, to the belief that they could find a way out, together.

Myrdian staggered back, his eyes wide with shock as the magic surged, the very ground beneath them cracking and splitting. The dark energy that had surrounded them began to dissipate, pushed back by the force of their love, the strength of their bond. Liora's heart pounded as she felt the curse retreat, its grip loosening, but the pain—the pain in her chest—was still there. Still clawing at her, trying to drag her into the darkness.

Thorne's hands gripped her tightly, his voice breaking as he tried to hold onto her. "Liora, stay with me. Please."

She could feel his love, his fear, his desperate need to save her, and it was enough. It was everything she needed to keep fighting, to keep pushing back against the curse.

"We'll do this together," she whispered, her eyes locked on his. "We're not giving up. Not now."

And as the last of Myrdian's magic began to dissipate, the figure stepped back, his face contorted with rage. "You think you've won?" he hissed. "This isn't over. The curse will claim you both—*no matter what.*"

But Liora, her hand still clasped tightly in Thorne's, felt a flicker of hope. The curse had not won. Not yet. And they would not stop fighting. Not for anything.

The bond between them remained unbroken, a thread of light in the darkness, and they would hold onto it, no matter the cost.

Eleven

The Thorned Betrayal

The sky above was a swirl of dark clouds, a storm on the verge of breaking. The air was thick with tension, the world holding its breath as if waiting for the inevitable. The clearing, where they had stood only moments ago, now seemed like a place of death, a place where life had once flourished but was now tainted by darkness. The wind carried a bitter chill, the trees swaying violently as if reacting to the power in the air. Myrdian was gone, for now, his presence lingering like a suffocating fog, and yet, the weight of his offer remained, pressing on Liora's chest like a stone.

She stood beside Thorne, their hands clasped tightly, but the bond between them—once their strength, once their salvation—had turned into a fragile thread, one that could snap at any moment. Her heart was torn between him and the terrible promise that Myrdian had made.

"How much longer can we fight this, Liora?" Thorne's voice

was hoarse, his words filled with exhaustion and despair. He was fading in front of her, his body breaking down under the curse's relentless grip. His once-vibrant eyes were now clouded with pain, his strength almost gone. He had fought for her, fought for them, but Liora knew that even his will to survive was starting to crumble.

"Thorne…" Liora whispered, her voice barely audible, as though saying the words aloud would shatter her completely. She had known for so long that the curse was a living thing, a presence between them, but now the cost of it felt too high. The decision that Myrdian had offered her—the terrible, twisted choice to save him, to save them both—was like a knife at her throat.

The promise to destroy the curse was within her reach. But only if she gave herself to Myrdian. Her soul. Her body. Willingly.

She could feel the weight of it in every fiber of her being, the curse pulling tighter, gnawing at her, trying to break her resolve. The thorns in her chest throbbed with a sickening intensity, a constant reminder of the bargain she was being asked to make. And yet, Thorne was beside her, the one person who had always stood by her, and he was fading. She could feel the bond between them stretching thin, threatening to snap with every second that passed.

"Please, Liora," Thorne said, his voice raw. "Don't let him win. Don't give in. You're the only one who can save us. *You're the only one who can save me.*"

Her breath caught in her throat, the weight of his plea like a heavy stone in her chest. She wanted to say she could save him, that together, they could find a way. But every time she tried to imagine a future without the curse, the price of it—a price she might have to pay—grew steeper, darker.

"Thorne," she began, but her voice faltered. She couldn't even bring herself to say it. The words that had once seemed like a promise now felt like a death sentence. "If I give myself to him… if I let him take me, he'll destroy the curse. We'll be free."

Thorne's face twisted with confusion and horror. "You don't mean that," he said, a tremor in his voice. "You can't. *You* can't—"

"I have to," Liora interrupted, her voice trembling with the weight of the truth. "I can't lose you, Thorne. But I can't let you die either. And Myrdian… Myrdian says this is the only way."

His grip on her hand tightened, desperation flashing in his eyes. "No. No, you don't understand. The curse may take me, but I would rather die than lose you like that. *You* are worth more than anything. *You* are worth fighting for. Not like this."

Liora felt the thorns twist deeper, their jagged edges slicing at her heart, making her gasp for air. Every word Thorne spoke tore her apart, a reminder that their love—so pure, so beautiful—was bound by chains that neither of them could escape. She wanted to fight it. She wanted to believe that there was a way out, a way for them both to survive. But each passing moment, each flare of agony from the curse, made it harder to hold onto that hope.

"I can't lose you either, Thorne," Liora whispered, her tears threatening to spill as she reached for him, her fingers trembling. "But what am I supposed to do? How can I live with myself, knowing you're suffering? Knowing that this curse is killing you?"

His eyes softened, his hand coming to her face, gently

brushing away the tears that had begun to fall. "I don't want you to sacrifice yourself. We'll find another way. Together."

Liora closed her eyes, letting the words wash over her. Together. *Together.* The very word felt like a lifeline. But how could she ask him to bear the weight of the curse for both of them? How could she be so selfish?

She looked into his eyes, her heart breaking with every word she spoke. "I… I don't know if I can let you go through this. I don't know if I can watch you die."

But before he could respond, a voice cut through the air—a voice so familiar, so full of malice, that it sent a cold shiver down Liora's spine.

"I see you've made your decision."

Liora froze, her heart skipping a beat as the shadow of a figure emerged from the darkened trees. It was a figure she had not seen in far too long, yet one whose presence had haunted them both—one who had sworn loyalty to Thorne's family.

Sorin.

He stepped forward, his face drawn with tension, his eyes betraying a mixture of regret and something else—something darker, more calculating. The shadows around him seemed to bend, as if the very earth itself was recoiling from his presence.

"Sorin," Thorne whispered, his voice barely audible. "What are you doing here?"

Sorin's lips curved into a thin smile. "I'm here to make sure you don't make a mistake, Thorne. You're *both* running out of time."

Liora could feel her heart racing, her blood running cold. Sorin—her closest ally, the one she had trusted above all others—was standing before them, a stranger now. A betrayer.

"You've been working with Myrdian?" Liora said, her voice

barely a whisper, the betrayal cutting deeper than she could have ever imagined.

Sorin nodded slowly, his gaze flickering toward Thorne before returning to Liora. "You think I didn't know about the curse? You think I didn't know what would happen? I have watched you both struggle, watched you fall into this trap. The curse is not just a thing of magic, Liora. It's a tool. And Myrdian—he's not wrong. *This is the only way to stop it.*"

Thorne stepped forward, his body trembling with anger and disbelief. "You *sold* us out? After everything, Sorin? You were supposed to be my friend. You swore your loyalty to me!"

Sorin's smile faltered, and for the first time, there was a flicker of regret in his eyes. "I didn't have a choice, Thorne. My loyalty was to your family, to the throne. To the power that comes with it. The curse has always been a weapon. And now, we can use it. We can end it *together.*"

Liora felt the ground beneath her feet shift, her breath coming in ragged gasps as she processed Sorin's words. Betrayal. Power. She had known, deep down, that there was something off about him, something he was hiding. But to hear him admit it—*to hear him admit he had been working with Myrdian*—shattered her. Everything she had believed in, everything she had trusted, was a lie.

"You… You've been manipulating us all along?" she asked, her voice shaking with anger and betrayal. "All of this—*everything*—it was a game to you? To get power?"

Sorin's gaze softened, and for a fleeting moment, Liora thought she saw the man she had once trusted, the Sorin who had stood by her. But it was gone, replaced by the cold, calculating look of someone who had made a choice, and who now saw the consequences of that choice in a different light.

"Yes," he said quietly. "I did what I had to do. To survive. And now, you have a choice, Liora. You can give yourself to Myrdian. You can save Thorne. Or you can let him die. But remember, I didn't come here to *rescue* you. I came here to make sure *you* made the right choice."

Liora's chest tightened with an unbearable pressure, the weight of his words sinking deep into her bones. Sorin's betrayal was one thing, but the realization that she was being forced to choose between saving Thorne and saving herself was too much to bear. The curse had already torn them apart, and now, it seemed, the choice was hers. She could not save both of them. Not without losing herself.

She turned to Thorne, her heart breaking as she saw the pain in his eyes. His weakness—his suffering—was all she had wanted to stop. And yet, in this moment, it seemed that nothing could save them. Nothing but the price she was willing to pay.

"I…" Liora began, her voice trembling as she looked at Sorin, and then back at Thorne. "I don't know if I can do this. I don't know what to choose anymore."

Thorne stepped closer, his hand reaching for hers, his grip warm but weak. "We face this together, Liora," he said softly. "No matter what happens. Together."

But deep in her heart, Liora knew. The choice had already been made for her. The question was not if she could save them both, but if she was willing to sacrifice everything she had ever known—her love, her soul—*to save him.*

And the price for that salvation was a cost she wasn't sure she could pay.

As Sorin's shadow loomed over them, Liora knew one thing above all else: *Whatever happened next, it would change everything.*

Liora stood in the heart of the clearing, the dark weight of Sorin's words pressing down on her. The wind had stilled, and the shadows seemed to lengthen, growing darker and colder with each passing moment. Myrdian's influence was still thick in the air, like a fog that couldn't be shaken. She could feel it tightening around her heart, like a vice slowly squeezing the life from her. And yet, despite the pain of the curse, despite the rage burning inside her, there was something else she could feel—a whisper, barely audible, that pulled her deeper into the storm.

She turned to Thorne, whose pale face betrayed the exhaustion of a thousand battles fought within his body, his eyes dim with the weight of the curse. His hand, still gripping hers, was warm, but growing weaker, and she could feel the pulse of his life, erratic and fragile, through the bond between them.

"Thorne," she whispered, her voice trembling, though she was determined to hold her ground. "I—I can't… I don't know if I can make this choice."

He stepped closer, his breath shallow, but his eyes remained steady, unyielding in their love for her. He reached up to cup her face, his touch gentle despite the strain in his body. "Liora," he murmured, his voice breaking with emotion. "I'm not asking you to sacrifice yourself. I'm asking you to *believe* in us. In *our* strength. This curse, this dark magic, it thrives on fear and isolation. You can't let it tear you apart. Don't let it make the decision for you."

She closed her eyes at the sound of his words. She wanted to believe him. She wanted to believe that they could overcome this, that their love could defeat the curse. But every time she looked at him, every time she felt the growing strength of the curse within her, she was torn. The power that Myrdian offered—freedom, salvation for Thorne—was so close, within her grasp. But the cost… it was too high.

Sorin's cold voice cut through the air, as though sensing her hesitation, sensing her conflict. "You can't save him, Liora. Not like this. And Myrdian's offer? It's the only way for you both to live."

Liora flinched at his words, but she refused to turn toward him. Sorin's betrayal, his shifting allegiances, had shattered her trust in him. The man who had once been her closest ally, her confidant, was now the harbinger of her deepest fears. He had already chosen the path of power and manipulation. He had chosen to align himself with the darkness that sought to devour them both.

"You've made your choice," Liora said, her voice a low, almost guttural growl, filled with disbelief and sorrow. "You've *sold* us out. You betrayed us for what? Power? Control?"

Sorin's expression didn't change, his face cold and un-readable, but there was something else there—a flicker of something buried deep beneath his icy demeanor. Perhaps regret. Or maybe, in the end, even he was just a victim of the same curse, the same hunger for power that had destroyed so many before him.

"I didn't betray you, Liora," Sorin said, his voice growing cold and distant. "I'm giving you a choice. A way out. You can save him, if you sacrifice yourself. But don't kid yourself—*that* is the true cost of this curse. Your love, your life. And you'll save him from his suffering."

Thorne's hand clenched tighter around Liora's, pulling her back toward him, his voice filled with desperation. "Liora, no.

I don't want you to give yourself to him. I would rather die than see you fall into his hands, his power. Don't you dare let him make this choice for you."

Tears welled in Liora's eyes as the weight of it all crashed down on her. Every piece of her was caught in a storm of love, fear, and regret. The bond between them—the curse, the promise of freedom—was pulling her in opposite directions. The thought of losing Thorne tore her apart, but the thought of losing herself, of becoming something she was not, was equally unbearable.

Her breath came faster as her hands pressed against her chest, the thorns twisting painfully inside her. The pain was unlike anything she had felt before. It was as if her very soul was being torn apart, and she felt a crushing pressure in her chest, a sense of suffocating darkness wrapping around her.

"Thorne…" she whispered, her voice barely audible as her fingers gripped his tighter. "I—I don't know if I can *keep* doing this. I don't know if I can watch you die. I can't lose you."

His eyes softened, and despite the strain in his voice, there was a flicker of something bright, something enduring that reached out to her. "Then don't lose me," he said, his voice fierce, unwavering. "We'll find another way. We can fight this. You don't have to sacrifice yourself, Liora. Not for me. Not for this curse."

The air around them seemed to vibrate with the weight of their words. Myrdian's power, the dark energy still thick in the clearing, pulsed as though it were alive, feeding off the conflict between them. Sorin stood to the side, watching them with an unreadable expression, his hands clenched at his sides as if anticipating the moment of their decision.

"You think you have time, don't you?" Sorin said, his voice

low and insistent. "You think you can resist the inevitable. But you can't, Liora. Not when Thorne's life is hanging in the balance. *You* are the only one who can save him now. You're running out of options. You *know* that."

The weight of his words crushed her. She could feel it deep in her soul. The curse was slipping through her fingers, like sand, and soon, it would be too late.

A cold wind swept through the clearing, rustling the trees and making the shadows dance around them like living things. Liora looked up at Thorne, his face pale, his lips parted with the effort of breathing. His body had been failing him for so long. How much longer could he hold on?

Sorin took a step forward, sensing her weakening resolve. "This is it, Liora. You can either sacrifice everything you've known to save him, or you can watch him die. *Make the choice.*"

Her breath hitched in her throat, her chest tightening with each word Sorin spoke. She could see Thorne's face, the desperation in his eyes as he searched her expression, as though he were trying to make her understand. His love for her was undeniable. It was all-consuming, and it was the very thing that had kept them together all this time.

But now, that love seemed to be the source of their destruction.

She closed her eyes, feeling the weight of the choice pressing on her. The thorns in her chest burned, each breath feeling like a blade digging deeper. She couldn't do this. She couldn't bear to choose between him and herself.

"I can't," Liora whispered, her voice breaking as tears streamed down her face. "I can't *lose* you."

Thorne stepped closer, his voice gentle but firm. "Then don't. Fight with me, Liora. We fight this together."

But before she could respond, a sharp crack split the air, the earth trembling beneath them as a figure emerged from the darkness—a figure they both recognized instantly. It was a man they had both trusted, someone who had once fought beside them in battles long past.

The figure moved with terrifying speed, his blade drawn, his eyes burning with something darker than any of them had anticipated.

Sorin.

Liora's blood turned cold. What had he done?

Sorin stepped forward, his sword raised in a strike that was both swift and precise. Thorne's eyes widened with horror, but it was too late.

Liora screamed in shock and horror as Sorin's blade struck Thorne with deadly force.

"No!" Liora cried, falling to her knees as the world around her blurred. She reached out, desperate to catch Thorne before he fell.

But Sorin stood between them now, his eyes cold, the betrayal evident in every movement. "You should have chosen, Liora," Sorin said softly, his voice devoid of regret. "You should have chosen *me*."

Thorne's body crumpled to the ground, a pool of blood forming beneath him. Liora's chest constricted, the pain almost unbearable as she felt his life slipping away.

"Thorne!" Liora screamed, her heart breaking, her soul shattering into pieces.

But Sorin stepped back, his sword raised in victory, his cold eyes gleaming with the knowledge of his betrayal. "He was never meant to survive," he said quietly, his voice filled with finality.

Liora's world crashed down around her, the thorns in her chest twisting as her own heart seemed to break in two. The love that had once felt like a sanctuary now felt like the greatest curse of all. And as she knelt there, staring at the bloodstained ground beneath her, she realized that the cost of her choices had just become a reality—one she would never be able to undo.

Thorne was slipping away.

And Liora was left with nothing but the consequences of her choices, the agony of her decisions threatening to consume her completely.

She was *too late*.

And the pain of that realization would haunt her forever.

Twelve

The Heart's Flame

The moon hung high above the ruins, casting its pale light through the gnarled branches of the trees surrounding the ancient temple. Liora's pulse thundered in her ears as she stood over Thorne, her hands trembling, her heart aching with every beat. The blood that stained the ground beneath them was a vivid reminder of the price they had paid for love. Sorin's betrayal had left them broken, and now, as Thorne's breath came slower and more shallow with each passing moment, it felt as though they were both teetering on the edge of annihilation.

She looked down at him, her mind racing, her heart beating with a frantic rhythm. There had to be a way to save him. There had to be something she could do to break the curse before it consumed them both. She could feel it in her chest—the pressure, the weight of the thorns that had been embedded deep within her, like living vines of agony that reached into her very soul. It was killing her. And it was killing him too.

Thorne's eyes fluttered open, his gaze unfocused at first, and then, as if reaching for something to ground him, his hand reached out toward her, his fingers brushing her skin. She caught his hand, her throat tight as the love between them pulsed like a living thing, the bond that had been their curse now their only remaining strength.

"I'm here," she whispered, her voice breaking. "You're going to be okay. I'll fix this. I promise."

Thorne's lips parted in a strained attempt to speak, but the words didn't come. Instead, his eyes darkened, his body convulsing slightly, as though the curse was attempting to drag him back into the darkness. His chest rose in a painful gasp, his body trembling with the effort of holding onto life.

Liora's own body burned with the strain of the thorns inside her. They seemed to writhe, alive, pressing harder against her ribcage as if to remind her of what was at stake. She could feel the ancient power pulsing beneath the temple's stones— the forbidden magic that had always been a part of the curse, waiting for someone to claim it. She had always avoided it, knowing its dangers. But now, desperate, her love for Thorne a roaring inferno in her chest, she knew there was no other choice.

If she didn't act now, she would lose him.

The forbidden magic was the only thing that could save them. The only way to break the curse once and for all.

Liora's hands shook as she rose to her feet, her eyes darting to the ancient altar where the runes glowed faintly in the darkness. The power in the room was thick, almost suffocating. It called to her, luring her forward, offering its strength in exchange for her soul.

She turned her eyes back to Thorne, whose chest rose with a painful, ragged breath. His face was pale, his expression drawn with the agony of the curse. She couldn't lose him. Not like this.

"Please," she whispered to herself, though it felt as if the very ground beneath her was trembling in response. "I'll do anything."

Taking a deep breath, Liora stepped away from Thorne and approached the altar. The stone beneath her feet felt slick with the moisture of centuries-old magic, and she could feel the ancient presence wrapping around her, reaching into her bones like a cold, familiar hand. The thorns inside her writhed, responding to the call of the temple's dark power.

She placed her palms flat against the altar's surface, feeling the heat radiating from it as if the stone itself were alive. The runes carved into its surface began to glow brighter, the ancient symbols shifting and changing, pulsating with a rhythm of their own. Liora's heart beat faster, fear and resolve mixing within her. She knew what she was about to do—she was about to tap into a force she didn't fully understand, a magic older than anything she had ever encountered. And there was no going back.

"I have to do this," she muttered to herself, her voice barely audible over the pounding of her heart. "I have to save him."

And then, she did it.

The moment her hands touched the stone, the surge of power coursed through her like fire, searing her skin and racing through her veins. The thorns inside her flared with pain, twisting and shifting in response to the magic, and for an instant, Liora thought she might collapse under the intensity of it. Her breath caught in her throat, her body trembling with the force of the ancient energy that flooded her.

But she didn't let go. She held on.

The air around her seemed to vibrate with the sheer force of the magic, the temple itself alive with power. The light from the altar grew brighter, bathing the room in an eerie, otherworldly glow. The very walls seemed to pulse, as if they were breathing, the ancient magic within them awakened by her touch.

Liora could hear Thorne's breath behind her, shallow and labored. The bond between them flared painfully, the love they shared twisting and turning inside her. She could feel his pain, his desperation, and she knew that if she didn't act quickly, she would lose him.

The magic surged again, rushing through her like an unstoppable wave. The thorns in her chest dug deeper, the pain becoming unbearable, but Liora refused to let go. She could feel the curse pulling at her—its tendrils reaching for her soul, but she fought it, clinging to the love that had always kept her grounded.

Then, the altar's power began to shift, to change. It was as though the ancient magic had found its way into her very soul, and the connection between her and Thorne deepened. A pulse of light erupted from the altar, shooting into the air like a beacon, and Liora screamed, her voice raw with the intensity of the magic.

Thorne's voice came then, weak and desperate. "Liora!"

She turned toward him, her body swaying with the overwhelming power that surged within her, and saw the desperation in his eyes. But it wasn't just desperation. It was something deeper. Something stronger.

The bond between them was no longer a curse. It was a *force*.

Thorne's body trembled as he pushed himself to his knees, his face twisted with pain, but there was something else there too—something powerful and undeniable. His love for her.

Liora reached for him, her body shaking with the power coursing through her. But as she did, the magic flared, a violent burst of energy erupting from her chest, tearing through the room like a thunderclap.

"No!" she cried, feeling the bond between them snap tighter, pulling her forward. "Thorne, no!"

But it was too late.

Thorne, in a desperate act of love, reached out, grabbing her hands as the magic surged between them. The force of it was overwhelming, a wave of pure, raw power, and for a moment, Liora couldn't breathe. She felt herself being pulled into the storm, the magic spinning around them, binding them together in ways she couldn't have imagined. The curse, the darkness that had loomed over them for so long, seemed to tear at the edges of their connection.

And then, it happened.

The magic inside them—fueled by their love—exploded in a violent burst of energy. The temple shook, the stones groaning as if the very foundations of the world were trembling beneath the force of their bond. Liora's vision blurred, the world spinning around her as the power overwhelmed her senses.

But amid the chaos, something shifted. The curse—no longer a force of destruction—began to unravel. The dark tendrils that had wrapped around her heart loosened, fading into the air like smoke. The thorns that had once dug into her chest pulled free, leaving only the raw, aching sensation of the bond they had formed.

She could feel the curse fading, its hold on her and Thorne

slipping away.

In that moment, as the world around them swirled with light and shadow, Liora understood.

The love between them—the force that had been the source of their pain—was also the key to their salvation. It was the flame that could destroy the curse, burn through the darkness, and set them free.

But there was one more price to pay.

The power that surged between them was overwhelming, and Liora knew the truth. She could feel it deep in her bones, the way the magic *called* to her, urging her to make the final sacrifice. Her body burned with the intensity of it, and her mind reeled with the realization that, in the end, there was only one way to completely sever the curse.

She had to release her hold on him. She had to let go of the love that had bound them together.

"Thorne," she whispered, her voice trembling. "I have to do this. I have to *let go*."

Thorne's face twisted in confusion, in pain, but his voice was steady when he spoke. "No, Liora. Don't do this. We can survive this together. I won't let you go."

But Liora could feel the love between them intensifying, the power growing until it was more than she could control. She could feel herself being pulled apart by the energy, her very being unraveling in the storm of magic they had unleashed. But she held on to one thing, one truth—*this love was worth everything.*

"Thorne," she whispered, her voice cracking with the weight of the decision. "This is the only way."

And with that, she closed her eyes and released the final piece of herself—the part of her that had always been tied to him, to their love.

The world around them exploded in a burst of light.

The light surged around them like a living force, radiant and fierce, tearing through the air with a strength that seemed to shake the very foundations of the temple. Liora's heart raced as she felt the final remnants of her soul slip away, the love she had held for Thorne both the force that saved them and the final price she had to pay.

She gasped as the magic reached its peak, filling the clearing with blinding brilliance, then, just as quickly, it began to ebb. The force that had bound them together, the curse that had held them both captive for so long, seemed to fracture, its dark tendrils loosening from her body and from Thorne's. It was as if the magic had come alive with a mind of its own, breaking the curse apart, unraveling the dark chains that had entwined their fates. But even as it shattered, she felt herself begin to fade, a piece of her consciousness slipping away, like sand flowing through her fingers.

"Thorne…" she whispered, the words barely escaping her lips. Her vision blurred, and she could barely make out his form through the haze of light. She could see him reaching for her, his eyes wide with fear, his face twisted in anguish.

"Liora! Liora, no!" His voice cracked, sharp and desperate, and she felt the force of his love radiating toward her, but it wasn't enough. She could feel the bond between them beginning to dissolve, the energy of their connection surging one last time before it started to burn out.

She looked into his eyes, the love between them clearer than ever, and her heart broke all over again.

"Thorne," she breathed, her voice barely a whisper in the

growing silence. "We're free... You're free. The curse is... gone."

Her words were punctuated by a gasp as the last of the power surged through her, an explosion of light and warmth, before it all faded into nothing. The last thing she heard was Thorne's voice, his hands reaching for her, calling her name, desperate and raw.

Then, the light vanished.

The world around her went dark.

Liora opened her eyes, blinking against the bright sunlight that streamed through the cracks in the ancient temple walls. She was no longer standing before the altar, no longer surrounded by the pulse of magic that had nearly consumed her. Instead, she found herself lying on the ground, her chest heaving, her body aching as though she had been torn apart and sewn back together.

It was quiet.

For the first time in what felt like a lifetime, there was no pressure in her chest, no thorns twisting deep within her. The pain that had consumed her was gone, replaced by a strange emptiness that felt almost like freedom. Her fingers flexed against the cool earth beneath her, the sensation of life flooding back into her body with each breath.

"Liora."

Her name, whispered softly, brought her back to the present. She blinked rapidly, her vision still blurry, but she could make out a shape kneeling beside her, a familiar presence. Thorne. His face was pale, streaked with dirt and blood, but there was a spark in his eyes that hadn't been there before—hope. Relief.

He cupped her face gently, his touch warm against her cool skin. "Liora, you're awake. You're—" He faltered, his voice catching in his throat, and Liora saw the tears in his eyes before he could hide them. "You're really here."

She gasped, her breath shaking as she sat up, the weight of her own body feeling strange after everything she had been through. Her chest was free of the thorns, free of the agony that had been her constant companion. She could breathe without pain. She could *live*.

"Thorne," she said, her voice trembling, "you're… you're okay?"

His hand trembled as it reached for hers, and she could feel the warmth of his pulse, strong and steady. There was no sickness in him now, no sign of the curse that had ravaged him. His breath was steady, his eyes clear.

"I'm okay," he said softly, his voice still hoarse, but filled with relief. "We did it. The curse… it's broken."

Liora blinked, still trying to process the weight of his words. "But the price… I thought—" Her voice cracked, and she faltered for a moment, the memories of what she had done, what she had given up, flooding back like a tide.

"You saved me," Thorne interrupted gently, brushing her hair from her face. "You saved us both. I don't understand it all, but I know that whatever you did, it was worth it. You… you gave yourself to the magic, to that *power*, but I don't know what the cost was. I couldn't save you."

She pressed a hand to her chest, as if feeling for the remnants of the magic she had unleashed, but all that remained was a hollow space where the curse had been. She should have felt empty, as if she had lost a part of herself, but instead, she felt… whole. The love she had for Thorne was still there, undiminished, even though the magic that had bound them was gone.

Her voice was low, fragile as she spoke, the words tasting foreign in her mouth. "I thought I was going to lose you. But now..." She swallowed hard, trying to steady herself, her heart pounding with the realization of what she had done. "I did what I had to do. I gave the curse everything it wanted... and it took a piece of me in return. But you... you're free now. We're free."

Thorne shook his head, his brow furrowed as he looked down at her, his hands gentle but insistent on her shoulders, pulling her closer. "No. You didn't lose anything, Liora. You're still here. And that's all that matters to me. We'll figure the rest out. Together."

Tears welled in her eyes as she looked at him, seeing the raw emotion in his gaze—the love, the fear, the devotion that had always been there. And for the first time in what felt like forever, she allowed herself to feel it—really feel it. The weight of the sacrifice, of everything they had been through, began to settle within her, but so did the relief that they had survived. Together.

The world around them seemed to hold its breath as they sat there, facing each other in the ruins of the temple. The ancient stones that had once trapped them now lay silent, as if even the very air itself knew that the curse had been lifted. And yet, there was something else—something they both knew. They were no longer bound by the past. The curse had been a part of their lives, a constant shadow, but now they were free.

Thorne's hand reached up to cup her face once more, his thumb brushing the tear that had fallen. "I thought I was going to lose you forever," he whispered, his voice breaking with the weight of his words. "But now... now we can rebuild. Together."

Liora nodded slowly, a tear slipping down her own cheek as she realized just how much they had overcome. "Together," she echoed softly.

The world seemed to exhale around them, the storm of magic that had once threatened to consume them now fading into the distance, leaving only peace in its wake. For the first time, they were not fighting. For the first time, they were simply *together*.

And in that moment, as the moonlight bathed them both in its soft glow, Liora knew that they had won—not just over the curse, but over everything that had ever threatened to tear them apart.

They were free.

And nothing, not even the darkest magic, could take that away from them.

Thirteen

The Edge of Forever

The air was thick with the scent of rain. The storm had been brewing for hours, dark clouds swirling overhead, the heavens themselves preparing to unleash their fury. The wind howled through the trees, their branches swaying violently, as though they too felt the growing tension in the air. In the heart of the ancient forest, the final battle was about to begin. And Liora knew—*this* was the moment that would decide everything.

She stood at the edge of the clearing, the sacred space where they had once fought to free themselves from the curse. The ground was still marked with the echoes of magic—ancient, dangerous power that had once trapped them. But now, as she gazed out into the shadowed wilderness before her, it felt like they were walking into a different kind of storm. Myrdian was coming. And this time, there would be no way to run.

Thorne stood beside her, his presence a comforting weight

against her side. His hand, still warm despite the cold, was gripping hers tightly, as though he knew the weight of what lay ahead. His face was drawn, tired, but his eyes burned with the same fierce determination that had always driven him. He had been through so much. They had both been through so much. But they were still here, still standing, their hearts intertwined by love and sacrifice.

"I never imagined it would come to this," Thorne muttered under his breath, his voice low but filled with a mixture of dread and resolve. He looked out at the dark expanse ahead, his jaw tight. "I thought I could protect you, Liora. I thought we could find another way. But now—"

"You've already protected me more than you could ever know," she said softly, cutting him off. Her voice, though quiet, was full of conviction. She turned to face him, her hand coming up to cup his cheek, her thumb brushing against the faint stubble there. "We're in this together, Thorne. We always have been."

His gaze softened for a moment, his fingers tightening around her hand. "Together," he echoed, his voice almost as though he were convincing himself. "I never thought… never believed that *this* would be the price for us to be free. But here we are. And if this is the end… if we don't make it out of this, Liora, I need you to know… I love you. With everything I have."

A lump formed in Liora's throat at his words, and for a moment, the storm that raged around them, the looming battle with Myrdian, the very earth beneath their feet, all of it faded into the background. It was just the two of them, standing at the edge of forever, their love a beacon in the darkness.

But the moment was brief. The wind picked up again,

stronger now, and Liora felt a shiver race down her spine. The curse was still there, deep within her, twisting at the edges of her soul. It was dying—she knew that much—but not without a fight. Myrdian's dark forces were closing in, their shadows stretching across the land, threatening to choke the last remnants of hope from the world.

Liora exhaled sharply and straightened, her fingers curling into fists as her heart began to race. "We have no more time," she said. "He's coming. We need to be ready."

Thorne nodded grimly, his jaw set. "Then let's finish this."

They didn't speak after that. The quiet between them now wasn't filled with words, but with the weight of everything they had fought for. Everything they had survived. It was time to face Myrdian—head on. There was no running, no more bargaining. Only one path forward. One choice.

The wind howled again, and Liora felt a surge of magic that she couldn't explain. It was raw, wild, like a floodgate opening in her chest, and she knew—*this* was the power they would need. The curse that had once been their greatest enemy was now their most powerful weapon.

"Liora," Thorne said quietly, his voice filled with urgency. "Whatever happens… we fight this together."

"I know," she whispered, her heart tightening in her chest. "And we'll win. No matter what it takes."

Just as those words left her lips, a sudden crack of thunder split the sky, and the ground beneath them trembled. Myrdian's dark forces had arrived.

Liora didn't wait. She stepped forward, her eyes narrowing as she focused her energy, feeling the pulse of magic that surged inside her, that ancient power from the temple—the forbidden magic that had once torn her apart. But now, it felt like part of her, a force she could wield, a force that would tear through Myrdian's darkness if she could control it.

Thorne moved beside her, his hand on the hilt of his sword, his body tensed for the battle to come. They had no armor, no weapons of true power, only the love between them—and the magic that had bound them together. But for once, that was enough.

"Prepare yourself," Liora said, her voice steady, though the pounding in her chest was almost deafening. She could feel Myrdian's presence, a black, choking cloud that wrapped itself around the forest, a shadow that grew longer with each passing moment.

From the woods ahead, a dark figure stepped into the clearing. Myrdian.

He stood tall, his black cloak billowing in the wind, his eyes glowing with a sickly green light. The air around him shimmered with dark magic, an energy so heavy it seemed to distort reality itself. Liora could feel it pressing against her, trying to invade her thoughts, to take control of her mind. The last remnants of the curse, the last threads of their connection, were winding their way toward him.

And yet—Liora didn't flinch.

"Ah, the lovers are still standing," Myrdian's voice came, a hiss through the night. "How touching."

His lips curled into a cruel smile as he surveyed them both, his eyes flicking between Liora and Thorne. "You've done well to make it this far, but it ends tonight. The curse will not be broken. You cannot escape what has been set in motion."

"Then why are you here?" Thorne snarled, stepping forward, his sword drawn, his posture tense. "If it's truly over, why come now? Why not let us be free?"

Myrdian laughed darkly, his voice filled with mockery. "You think you're free? You're both fools. *Your love*—it's the key to the curse. You were always meant to die together, bound by it. All I've done is make sure that when the time comes, I will be the one to seize the power that should have been mine. This world, your world, will bow to me, *whether* you like it or not."

"You're wrong," Liora said, her voice sharp, filled with the strength of everything they had endured. She stepped forward, the power within her surging, her body crackling with the intensity of the magic that flowed through her. "We *won't* let you win."

Myrdian's gaze darkened, and the air around them seemed to freeze. "Then you will die first."

With a flick of his wrist, the dark magic surged toward them, a wave of energy so powerful that the ground beneath their feet cracked and splintered, sending a wave of force through the clearing. Liora raised her hand, summoning the power of the magic within her. She could feel the curse's tendrils swirling inside her, fighting for dominance, but she *forced* it back, letting only the pure energy of love and will surge through her.

The ground beneath her feet trembled as the magic collided, a shockwave that rattled her bones. The trees around them swayed violently, their leaves tearing free and swirling around them like leaves caught in a violent wind. The sky above seemed to open, as though the heavens themselves were torn apart by the violence of the battle.

Thorne's sword struck first, slashing through the dark magic, and though Myrdian's energy hissed in the air, crackling and burning, he didn't falter. The two forces collided again and again, each clash more intense than the last, each blow threatening to consume everything in its wake. Liora's magic and Myrdian's dark power locked together like two forces of nature, and the sheer energy threatened to tear the very world around them apart.

But Liora could feel it now. The curse was dying, unraveling, but she had to control it. She had to *take it*—and turn it back on him.

She raised her hands, focusing the energy, pulling the remnants of the curse into her. The love between her and Thorne pulsed through her like a lifeline, anchoring her to reality as the magic inside her swirled, chaotic and dangerous. It was her last chance to break the cycle, to destroy Myrdian's hold over them once and for all.

"You don't control me anymore, Myrdian!" Liora shouted, her voice ringing out through the chaos. "I *choose* my fate!"

With a final surge of power, Liora released the magic.

The force of it slammed into Myrdian, sending him stumbling back. His scream echoed through the clearing, his body writhing as the dark magic that had once bound him fell apart. The curse, no longer tethered to him, disintegrated, unraveling into nothingness.

Liora fell to her knees, exhausted, the remnants of the battle still crackling in the air, but the tension was gone. The curse was *gone

*.

Thorne was beside her in an instant, his arms wrapping around her, pulling her close as they both breathed, the weight of everything they had just done sinking in. Their hearts were still racing, but there was no more pain, no more darkness.

It was over.

They had won.

And as the storm clouds began to part, the moon breaking

through the darkness, Liora and Thorne knew one thing for certain: love had not only saved them—it had destroyed the curse forever.

The world around them was still as the echoes of the final clash faded into the night. The wind, once howling with fury, had stilled. The air, thick with the remnants of dark magic, hung heavy, but for the first time in what felt like forever, there was an overwhelming sense of calm. The storm that had raged inside them, and the storm that had threatened to consume their world, was no longer there.

Liora's heart was still racing, her breath coming in shallow gasps as the weight of everything settled into her bones. She was alive. Thorne was alive. They had survived.

But there was no time for rest.

Thorne's arms tightened around her, pulling her closer. "Are you okay?" His voice was a gentle whisper against her ear, laced with concern, but there was a tremor in it, a mixture of fear and relief.

She nodded, her face pressed against his chest as she tried to steady her breathing. Her hands gripped his shirt, the fabric cool beneath her fingers. Her body ached, exhausted from the intense power she had wielded, the magic still coursing through her veins, but it was nothing compared to the relief of being in his arms. The pain was fading, the curse gone, but the memory of everything they had been through lingered like an unspoken promise.

"I'm okay," Liora said, pulling away slightly to look up at him. "We did it, Thorne."

He looked down at her, his expression softening, but his eyes were still filled with the weight of their shared history, the trauma of what they had survived. "We did," he whispered, his thumb brushing against her cheek, wiping away the remnants of the tears she hadn't even realized had fallen. His lips parted, as if there was more he wanted to say, but his voice faltered, the magnitude of everything still settling on him.

The silence between them stretched, but it wasn't uncomfortable. It was the quiet that came after the storm, the quiet before the first steps into a new beginning.

But then, from the corner of her eye, she saw movement.

A shadow stepped forward from the edge of the clearing, and Liora tensed, instinctively stepping back from Thorne, her heart pounding. Her breath caught in her throat. For a moment, she feared that the battle wasn't over. That the curse, the dark forces, would come crashing back to claim them.

But it wasn't Myrdian.

It was someone else.

Liora's breath escaped her in a rush of disbelief as the figure stepped fully into the moonlight.

Sorin.

His face was bruised, his clothes torn, but it was unmistakable. He stood there, his eyes hollow, his posture slumped as though the weight of the world had finally crushed him.

For a long moment, Liora just stared at him, disbelief still warring with anger. Sorin, the one who had betrayed them both. The one who had turned his back on them for power. The one who had once sworn loyalty to Thorne's family—and to her.

But now, he stood before them, broken.

Thorne's hand, still holding Liora's, tightened. "Sorin," he said quietly, his voice laced with a mix of caution and fury. "What are you doing here?"

Sorin didn't immediately respond. He stood still, his gaze flickering between Liora and Thorne, as if weighing something heavy on his conscience. The moonlight cast long shadows across his face, highlighting the exhaustion that had settled into every line of his features. The magic that had once seemed to flow through him was gone, replaced by something more fragile, more human.

"I…" Sorin began, his voice rough and barely above a whisper. He took a slow, deliberate step forward. "I came to stop Myrdian. To undo what I helped him do."

Liora blinked, her heart suddenly pounding in her chest. "Stop him? After everything?" Her voice shook, the anger and betrayal bubbling to the surface once more. "You *helped* him. You *betrayed* us."

Sorin's eyes flinched, the weight of her words clearly hitting him. "I didn't mean for it to go this far," he said, his voice breaking, his words almost a plea. "I thought—when Myrdian promised me power, when he said he could help me take control, I thought it was the only way. I thought I could control the darkness, manipulate it to my will. But when I saw what was happening to you, what was happening to Thorne…" He trailed off, his voice cracking. "I couldn't stand by anymore. I couldn't keep lying to myself."

Thorne stepped forward, his expression unreadable. "You've already done enough damage, Sorin," he said coldly, his voice steely. "How many lives did you cost in your *quest* for power?"

Sorin's face twisted in pain, the regret evident in his eyes. "I know," he whispered. "I know. And I would undo it if I could, but there's no going back. I was wrong. I was a fool."

Liora stood motionless, her heart torn. A part of her wanted to scream at him, to rage against him for the lies, for the betrayal. For all of it. But another part—the part that had known him, the part that had once trusted him—saw the vulnerability in his eyes, the admission of the hollow, broken man standing before her. She wasn't sure if she could forgive him. She wasn't sure if she wanted to.

But she couldn't forget what they had shared.

"What do you want, Sorin?" she finally asked, her voice sharp, yet filled with a deep weariness. "Why are you here now?"

Sorin's gaze dropped to the ground for a moment, the weight of her question sinking deep into his chest. When he looked back up, his eyes were heavy, filled with something more than regret.

"To *help*," he said softly, the word almost foreign on his lips. "I can't undo what I did. But I can help you destroy Myrdian. He's not finished. He's not done with you. You have to be ready."

The words hung in the air between them, a harsh reality setting in. Liora felt the air grow heavier, the tension in the clearing thickening with each passing second. The night was still, yet the storm was not over.

Thorne turned to face Liora, his brow furrowed, his jaw set. "Do we trust him?"

Liora didn't answer immediately. Her eyes flickered to Sorin, to the man who had once been her friend, who had once shared her dreams and her fears. She remembered the way he had stood by her side, the way they had fought for their cause together. But the man who stood before her now was not the man she had known. He was a shadow of what he once was, and in many ways, she wasn't sure she could ever forgive him.

But Thorne—*Thorne*—was still her everything. And their love, their bond, had always been stronger than anything else.

"I don't know," Liora said finally, her voice steady despite the storm in her chest. "But we don't have a choice. We can't let Myrdian win."

Sorin nodded slowly, as if accepting her decision. "Then we have no time to waste," he said. "I can help you defeat him. But you need to understand… Myrdian's power is far stronger than you think. It's bound to him. It's bound to the curse you both fought so hard to break. This fight isn't over—not by a long shot."

Liora glanced back at Thorne, her heart in turmoil. This was the moment—the moment they had fought for. They were so close, so close to freedom. But they had to be ready.

Thorne nodded, his gaze unwavering. "We're ready."

Sorin stepped back, giving them space. The moment between them was thick with the understanding that there would be no turning back. Whatever happened next would be their final battle—the battle that would either break them or set them free.

Liora took a deep breath, feeling the weight of everything they had been through, everything they had fought for, pressing down on her. Thorne squeezed her hand, and for the first time in what felt like forever, she felt something else—*hope*.

No more lies. No more manipulation. This was their moment. Their love, once their greatest weakness, had now become their greatest weapon.

Together, they could face the storm. Together, they could defeat Myrdian.

And as the first drops of rain began to fall, the storm finally broke, and Liora and Thorne stepped forward into the unknown, ready to face whatever came next.

Ready to face the edge of forever.

Fourteen

The Sacrifice

The wind howled through the trees, whipping against their faces, as if nature itself sought to drown out the storm building in their hearts. The world felt on the verge of breaking. Shadows stretched long and ominous in the fading light, dark clouds swirling above them, blocking the last vestiges of the dying day. The air was thick with magic—dangerous, suffocating power, crackling like static, charged with the raw energy of a battle that would define the future of everything they loved.

Liora stood at the edge of the battlefield, her eyes locked on Thorne. He was only a few steps away, but it felt like miles. His face was grim, sweat dripping down his brow, and the hand that gripped his sword shook ever so slightly. His chest rose and fell in sharp, rapid breaths. They had fought together through hell and back, and now, this—this was the final confrontation.

Myrdian stood before them, his presence darker than anything Liora had ever known. The man, once a shadow in her life, was now the embodiment of the curse. His black cloak billowed around him, the edges of it seeming to dissolve into the shadows themselves. His eyes glowed with that sickly green light that had haunted them for so long.

"You've come so far," Myrdian said, his voice low, filled with dark amusement. "But you think you can defeat me now? You have no idea what you're truly up against."

Liora could feel the magic surging through her veins, the energy of the curse still deeply embedded in her, though it had been weakened. The bond that tied her to Thorne—the love, the pain, the agony—was stronger than ever. She could feel it in every part of her. But now, Myrdian's power was the greatest force they had ever encountered. She had known, from the beginning, that this battle was more than just the curse. It was the very essence of what they had become. Love, loss, and sacrifice.

"No," Liora said, her voice firm, despite the terror curling in her chest. "You're wrong. We will defeat you."

Myrdian's lips curled into a sneer, but there was no amusement there—only the cold, calculating certainty of someone who believed in their own power. "You think your love can save you? Do you think that's enough to undo the curse I've put on you both?"

Her eyes flicked to Thorne, who stood a few feet away, his jaw clenched, his stance defensive. He was struggling, his body clearly weakened by the curse's toll, but his will was as unshakable as it had ever been. He was ready to fight. And so was she.

"We're not fighting alone," Thorne said, his voice a low rumble, full of determination. "We've already faced worse.

And we *won't* let you win."

Myrdian's laughter was soft, almost musical in its cruelty. "Do you even understand what you're up against? The curse was never just about *you two*. It was about controlling the very balance of life and death itself. And now…" He took a step forward, his voice dropping to a whisper. "Now it's time to finish it."

With a flick of his hand, the ground beneath them trembled, the very earth rumbling as if to shake them loose from their feet. Liora's breath caught in her throat as dark tendrils of magic twisted up from the earth, wrapping around her ankles and pulling at her limbs.

"Liora!" Thorne shouted, his voice urgent, his feet shifting as he tried to reach her. But the darkness was everywhere now, clawing at her, pulling her into the depths of the curse's power.

She struggled against it, the pressure growing with each passing second, the tendrils of black magic twisting like snakes around her legs, her arms, her chest. It was suffocating, consuming. She felt herself being pulled into the very heart of Myrdian's dark power.

"No!" she cried out, her voice raw, filled with defiance. "You won't win."

Her body burned as the magic twisted inside her, the curse fighting to take hold of her once more. The love she felt for Thorne surged, but it was tangled with a raw, desperate pain that threatened to tear her apart.

She reached out to Thorne, her hand desperate to find his, but the dark tendrils held her tighter. Her chest tightened, and the world seemed to shift, spinning into chaos as the power of the curse surged within her. She could feel the very edges of her soul unraveling, as though the very force of the curse was trying to take away everything that was her.

"Thorne, I can't hold on much longer!" Liora gasped, her breath coming in shallow bursts. The pressure was too much.

But Thorne—*Thorne*—was not letting her go. He fought the darkness with everything he had, his sword raised, the steel gleaming in the faint light. He slashed through the air with a cry of fury, cutting down the tendrils that reached for him, but they kept coming, the darkness never letting up.

"*We will* win, Liora," he shouted, his voice rising above the chaos. "We fight together. Always."

And then, as if he could hear the very essence of the curse calling out to him, Liora realized with a sickening certainty that there was one final choice they had to make. A choice neither of them could escape.

Her heart broke, and the magic inside her flared with a terrifying intensity. She knew. She knew what had to be done.

"Thorne," she whispered, her voice trembling, filled with a kind of sorrow that threatened to consume her. "I love you. You have to live. You have to survive."

Thorne's gaze flickered to her, his eyes wild with confusion and fear. "What are you talking about, Liora? No, we *do this together.*"

But she shook her head, feeling the pulse of the curse tightening its grip on her heart. She could feel the love between them burning brighter than anything she had ever known, but it was also pulling them closer to the darkness. The curse—this dark magic—was a force neither of them could outrun. And in that moment, Liora knew what must be done.

She reached out to him, her hand trembling as she grasped his. The magic surged between them, a storm of raw, unfiltered emotion. "Thorne," she whispered again, her voice filled with the agony of the decision. "If we're to defeat him… one of us must die. The curse cannot be undone otherwise. It has to end with one of us."

"No," Thorne cried, his eyes wide with disbelief. "I won't let you do this. We can find another way—there's always another way."

Liora could barely breathe through the pain, through the intensity of the love that surged within her. She could feel Thorne's heart, the pulse of his soul, as if it were her own. They were connected. They had always been connected. But now, she knew that the only way to break the curse and free them both was to make the ultimate sacrifice.

"Thorne, this is the only way," she said, her voice breaking. "You have to live. You *will* live. I'll stay behind. I'll make sure you survive. I can feel it inside me—the curse needs one of us. You're stronger. You're meant to live."

His face twisted with disbelief, his eyes filled with raw anguish. He reached for her, but the dark tendrils of magic tightened around her limbs, pulling her further into the heart of the curse. Liora cried out, but there was no strength left in her to fight the force that was consuming her.

"You can't make me choose, Liora," he said, his voice cracked with emotion. "You can't leave me."

"I love you," Liora whispered through the tears, her heart shattering in her chest. "And you'll carry me with you. Always."

With those words, Liora's body surged with a final, raw burst of magic, the force of their love overwhelming the curse. The dark tendrils that had held her began to unravel as the light of her sacrifice spread through the clearing, sweeping away the darkness in a wave of pure energy.

But it was too much. The final act of love—of pure

selflessness—was breaking her apart. Her body felt as though it were being torn in two, the magic racing through her veins, devouring her from the inside out. She felt herself slipping, felt the last remnants of her consciousness fading.

Thorne's scream reached her ears, but it was distant now, as if the world itself were falling away.

And then, everything went silent.

The darkness receded. The storm broke. The curse was gone.

Liora woke to silence.

The world was still, impossibly still. Her body felt weightless, as though she were floating. She blinked, the bright light of a new dawn filtering through a gap in the trees. The pain was gone, the agony that had consumed her, the magic that had raged within her.

And then, she saw him.

Thorne stood before her, his face streaked with tears, his body trembling. But he was alive. His heart was still beating. He was breathing.

"Liora…" he whispered, his voice breaking. His hand reached for her, as though afraid to touch her, as though afraid she might vanish like the darkness.

Liora stood, feeling the warmth of the sunlight on her skin, the weight of her sacrifice settling over her like a gentle cloak. She was no longer part of the world she had once known.

Liora's heart ached with the sight of Thorne before her—his face torn with grief and confusion, his hands trembling as if he couldn't quite believe she was standing there. She could see the raw, desperate need in his eyes, the longing to pull her close, to never let go. But she knew what they had both just sacrificed, what had been lost and what had been gained.

She felt the connection between them, but it was different now. She was different. The magic that had once bound them was no longer the same, and with the curse undone, the bond had shifted, leaving her with a profound emptiness, yet a strange sense of peace.

"Thorne," she whispered, her voice strained, her throat tight. She reached out, her hand brushing against his, feeling the warmth of his skin as his fingers closed around hers. She could feel the pulse of his heartbeat beneath her touch. *He was alive.* The curse that had stolen so much from them, the darkness that had threatened to tear them apart, was finally gone.

But at what cost?

Liora's breath caught as she looked at him, the love that had once felt like an unbreakable chain between them now seemed to be tinged with an unbearable sadness. The sacrifice she had made—the choice she had forced upon them both—hung in the air between them like a dark cloud.

"Liora…" Thorne's voice cracked as he spoke her name, and he stepped forward, his eyes never leaving hers. His steps were hesitant, like he wasn't sure if he could believe she was really there, truly standing in front of him. "Liora, I—I thought I lost you. I thought—"

"I'm here," she whispered, her voice trembling with the weight of her own emotions. She wanted to reach for him, to pull him into her arms, but her body felt strangely detached, as if she were still floating between worlds. "I'm still here, Thorne. I'm still with you."

But as the words left her lips, she realized the truth of them. She wasn't fully with him anymore—not in the way they had once been. The connection they had shared, the love that had burned so brightly between them, was now a flickering ember, the warmth fading as her presence in this world grew fainter.

She felt herself slipping, her body and soul already stretched thin by the sacrifice she had made. She had given everything to break the curse, to save him, to make sure that he could live without the weight of their doomed love hanging over him. But in doing so, she had also given up her place in this world.

"Thorne," she said again, this time more urgently. Her voice was faint, fragile. "You have to let me go."

The words hit him like a physical blow. He froze, his breath hitching in his throat, his eyes wide as he took a step back, as if the very ground beneath his feet had just crumbled away. "No," he breathed. "No, I won't let you go. You can't do this. You can't leave me."

Liora's chest tightened, the familiar ache of love and loss surging within her. She could feel the bond between them stretching thin, but she knew it had already been severed. She had made the choice. And now, she had to live with it.

"I have to, Thorne," she said, her voice soft but resolute. "I've already given everything to save you. The curse is gone. The magic is gone. But so am I. I can't stay here anymore."

His face crumpled with pain, his lips trembling as though he were trying to hold back the devastation threatening to break free. "I can't—*I can't lose you again.*" His voice broke, the rawness in it like a knife in her chest.

"You haven't lost me, Thorne," she said gently, her voice filled with tenderness. "You've won. You're free. You can live without the curse. Without the burden."

"But at what cost?" he asked, his voice barely a whisper, as if the weight of the question threatened to crush him. "*You* are the cost, Liora. You are everything. Without you—what is the point of it all?"

Liora took a shaky breath, the pain in her chest too much to bear, and yet she knew it was the only path forward. She stepped closer to him, though her legs felt weak beneath her, the world around her growing hazy as if she were sinking into something dark and cold.

The sunlight that had once filled the clearing now seemed dimmer, as if the world itself was grieving with her. She reached out, her fingers grazing his face, her touch so light it was barely there. "Thorne… I would give anything to stay. But the magic we fought so hard to destroy—it's already taken too much. I've given everything. *And now it's your turn to live.*"

"No," Thorne said, shaking his head, his voice breaking with the weight of his pain. "I can't live without you. You *are* my life, Liora. You're my everything."

Tears welled in her eyes as she looked into his face, her heart breaking all over again. *How could she make him understand?*

"I will always be with you, Thorne," she whispered, her voice trembling, but filled with love. "In your heart. In your memories. You carry me with you, always. And that's enough. It has to be."

Her hand trembled as it rested against his chest, over his heart. She could feel it beating beneath her fingers, strong and steady, a reminder of everything she had fought for.

"I love you, Thorne. I always have." Her voice broke on the last word, the sound breaking her even further. "And I always will."

He shook his head again, his breath ragged. "No, no… please… don't leave me like this." His hands reached for her, pulling her close, his forehead pressed against hers. "Please. I need you. We need *us.*"

Liora's eyes closed for a moment as she allowed the last remnants of their love to fill her. She knew this was the end—the end of their story, the end of everything they had fought for. And yet, the love they had shared, the love they still shared, would live on. It would be the one thing that could never be taken from them.

"I'm so sorry," she whispered, her voice barely audible as she felt herself slipping away.

Thorne's arms tightened around her, his body shaking with the force of his grief, but it was too late. The magic that had been holding her together was fading, dissipating like smoke on the wind. She could feel herself pulling away, the world growing distant and cold. The ground beneath her felt softer, as though she were being drawn into the earth itself, sinking away from him.

And then, with one final, desperate breath, she let go.

The world exploded in a rush of light, a final burst of magic as their love collided, burning brighter than the sun, a force that reached beyond time, beyond death. Thorne's cry echoed in her mind, his voice a piercing note of agony that would haunt her forever. But even as she felt herself slip into the darkness, Liora knew that the love they had shared would never die.

And somewhere, in the depths of her soul, she felt the last whisper of his touch, the final brush of his lips against hers—a promise that, no matter what, they would be together again.

Somewhere.

Someday.

And so, with that love, Liora faded into the light.

Fifteen

The Final Thorn

The sun dipped low in the sky, casting its dying light across the battlefield, now eerily silent. The once-violent storm had dissipated, leaving behind an unnatural stillness that wrapped around the ruined landscape like a heavy shroud. Where the dark magic had swirled in chaotic tendrils just hours before, there was now only the faintest echo of its presence, fading as the last remnants of the curse crumbled to dust. The air felt different—lighter, almost—but the change was bitter.

Thorne stood alone in the clearing, his hand still gripping the hilt of his sword. He hadn't let go. Not yet. The metal was cold against his fingers, a sharp contrast to the warmth of the late afternoon sun. His armor was cracked and dented, covered in the marks of battle. His face was streaked with dirt, blood, and the dried salt of tears, but his eyes were empty. For all the destruction they had caused, for all the forces they had defeated, the weight of the moment was almost unbearable.

Liora was gone.

She had given everything—her heart, her soul, her very existence—so that he could live. So that they could be free.

But it was a freedom he could never enjoy.

He turned away from the ruins of the battlefield, his breath shallow, his heart still pounding in his chest, as though it couldn't fathom the emptiness inside him. Each step felt as though the ground itself was pushing back against him, unwilling to let him leave. The absence of Liora was a black hole, sucking the life out of everything he had known. The love that had once defined him, that had once been a bond so strong, so full of light, was now a memory. A dream.

The path before him was unclear. There was no longer a curse to fight, no enemy to defeat. Only silence.

The trees at the edge of the forest loomed before him, twisted and dark, their branches reaching out like skeletal hands. The forest had always been there, a constant presence. But now, it seemed to close in around him, as though the world itself had become a cage. The weight of the magic was gone, but in its place was an even heavier weight—the ache of loss.

Thorne couldn't remember when the last time was that he had truly felt alive, the last time he had let his heart fully beat without fear. Everything had been overshadowed by the curse, by the fight for survival, for love.

Now, that fight was over.

"Thorne," a voice called from behind him, soft, familiar, yet impossibly far away. He froze, his breath catching in his throat. His hand, still clutching the hilt of the sword, tightened, as though he could use its strength to anchor himself in the world.

He didn't turn. He couldn't. Not yet.

The voice came again, closer this time, carrying the faintest trace of wind with it. The words seemed to resonate in his chest, but they didn't feel real.

He still couldn't turn. The weight of his grief kept him rooted in place, like a statue carved from stone.

But then he felt the presence. The familiar warmth. The bond that had once been a tether between them, pulling them through every storm, through every moment of agony and joy.

A soft breath against his ear. "Thorne…"

With a strangled gasp, he whirled around, his hand flying to the hilt of his sword, but no blade met his hand. No enemy stood before him. Only a shadow.

Liora.

Her presence hung in the air, not in the form of her body, but in the soft, glowing essence that surrounded her. It was her warmth, her light, the faint pulse of magic still left behind in the world—a lingering imprint that could never truly be erased. She was gone, but she was not *gone*.

She was still here. In the wind. In the rustling of the leaves. In the very air he breathed.

The grief that had consumed him—so sharp, so cold, so relentless—now felt like a distant ache, as if something deep inside him had shifted, a subtle change in the fabric of his soul. His eyes searched the trees around him, longing for something he knew he would never find, but also realizing that perhaps he had been looking in the wrong place all along.

His eyes burned with unshed tears, but no sound escaped him, no sobs, no cries. Just the quiet realization that Liora's sacrifice had meant more than the battle. More than the curse. It was the love they had shared, now sealed in the fabric of the universe. A love that could never truly be broken, not by death, not by time.

Thorne stood motionless, as the last light of the sun bled out across the horizon, the world falling into dusk. The stars began to appear in the sky, small pinpricks of light, shining bright against the darkening canvas above them. The breeze that blew through the trees carried with it the faintest scent of flowers, of earth, of life—and something more.

It was Liora's essence. He could feel it in his bones.

She was still here. Always.

He closed his eyes, exhaling slowly. The pain of loss, of love, was still there—but it no longer threatened to crush him. He could feel the warmth of her presence, the connection they had shared, the love that had flowed between them like a river— deep, fierce, unwavering. Even now, that love hadn't gone anywhere. It had become part of him, woven into the very threads of his being.

And that was enough.

As the first star blinked into existence above him, Thorne sank to his knees, the weight of everything settling around him. His heart, which had been shattered into a thousand pieces, was now pieced together by the memories of Liora. By the strength she had given him, by the love she had shown him, even in her final moments. She was with him, in his heart, in his soul, as he had always been with hers.

"Liora," he whispered, his voice raw, his chest aching with the weight of her name. "I will always carry you with me."

For a long moment, he remained on his knees, his head bowed, his hands clenched into fists at his sides. There was no more fight, no more magic. Just him. And her.

The wind whispered through the trees, and Thorne knew, without a shadow of doubt, that she was still here. Not in the way he had once known her, not in the form of her body, but in the love they had shared. That was the one thing that could never be broken. That was the one thing that would always remain.

As he stood, finally pulling himself to his feet, he felt the strength of her spirit within him. He had no idea what lay ahead. The world was so much different now—empty, almost. The curse was gone, but in its place was something else. Something… new.

But for the first time in what felt like forever, Thorne felt free. Not because the battle was over, but because he had learned that love wasn't something that could be taken from him. It wasn't something that could be destroyed by death, by time, or by dark forces.

And as the first night of their new world settled over him, Thorne knew one thing for certain: he would carry her memory for as long as he lived. He would hold her in his heart, a flame that would never go out. And when the time came for him to join her again, he would do so with love in his soul, knowing that they would never truly be apart.

For Liora, for the love they had shared, he would live.

And he would remember. Always.

Thorne stood there for a long time, the weight of Liora's absence still pressing heavily on his chest, but now, the feeling of her presence was growing clearer with each passing moment. The shadows that had once swallowed his heart seemed to be dissolving. A faint warmth lingered in the air around him—so soft, so delicate, but undeniably real. He closed his eyes and breathed deeply, feeling the coolness of the night air fill his lungs, the soft rustling of the trees above him carrying with it something faintly familiar.

In the distance, the soft hum of night insects began their song, the sound of life continuing as it always had. The quiet seemed different now. Thorne had become accustomed to the silence of loss, to the aching stillness of an empty heart. But now, there was something else. A quiet peace. A peace that was not without sorrow, but also without fear.

Slowly, he turned his gaze upward to the stars, the sky stretching above him in endless blackness, sprinkled with a million points of light. Liora's name echoed in his mind, a soft refrain that carried him forward, reminding him of the deep bond they had forged. That bond wasn't gone. Not completely. Even though the physical presence of her was no longer there, the energy they had shared—the love they had built—remained, woven into the very fabric of this world. And that was enough to keep him standing, enough to keep him breathing.

He hadn't realized until now how much of his life had been consumed by the curse. The darkness. The pain. Every step he had taken had been weighed down by it, by the constant pressure of an impending loss. But that weight had lifted. It wasn't just the curse that had bound him; it had been the fear of losing the one person who had given him strength. Liora. The one who had fought by his side, who had loved him fiercely even when he could barely love himself.

His breath hitched as memories flooded his mind. Her laugh. The way her eyes sparkled when she smiled. The quiet moments they had shared, sitting beneath the stars, hearts beating in sync, dreaming of a life without the curse. He felt it now—an ache, but also a warmth. A glow that had settled into the deepest parts of him, lighting up the dark corners of his soul.

He hadn't lost her.

Not truly.

Thorne turned and walked toward the edge of the forest, his pace slow but steady. His heart still ached, the loss of her too vast to comprehend in a single moment, but it was no longer the consuming force that it had once been. It was now a part of him. A part of the world that would always be with him, a quiet presence in the stillness of the night.

As he passed through the trees and made his way toward the open field that stretched beyond the forest, he could see the faint glow of the dawn breaking at the horizon. The first hints of light stretched across the sky, casting long shadows, illuminating the world in soft, golden hues. It felt as if the world itself had woken up, a new day beginning, unburdened by the curse that had once cast a shadow over everything.

Liora's sacrifice had broken the cycle. She had given everything, her life, her essence, to ensure he could live. And now, the world was free. Free of the curse. Free of the darkness that had threatened to choke the life from everything they had known.

Thorne could hear the faint call of birds overhead, the hum of life stirring in the trees and the grass beneath his feet. The world was still alive. It was still moving forward, as it always had. And as he stepped further into the field, he felt it—his connection to Liora, still strong, still tethered to his heart. It was not a painful connection anymore. It wasn't a burden. It was a gentle warmth that filled him with peace.

The first rays of sunlight kissed his face, the warmth seeping into his skin, and for the first time in so long, he felt hope stir within him. He was no longer bound by the curse. He was free. And so, in a way, was she.

Liora had always believed that their love could overcome anything. Even death. And now, as he stood alone in the quiet morning, Thorne could almost feel her beside him, walking with him through the world they had fought to save. He could hear her voice in the wind, feel the softness of her touch in the breeze that danced around him. The bond they had shared, though severed in the physical world, was not gone. It was eternal, written in the stars, in the fabric of the earth beneath his feet.

Thorne lowered his head, closing his eyes as the first rays of light bathed his face. His hands, still warm from holding the sword, now relaxed at his sides, the tension in his body easing for the first time in so long.

You will always be with me, he thought, his heart swelling with the truth of it. *You are the light in my heart. The fire that will never die.*

It was not the ending he had imagined. It wasn't the happy conclusion that he had once dreamed of. But it was the only one they had. The only one they could have. And in that truth, he found peace. Liora had given everything for him, and now, it was his turn to live—to live for the both of them.

And so he stood there, in the quiet of the morning, knowing that the road ahead was uncertain. That the world had changed, and that life—now free from the curse—was not always easy, but it was worth living. Liora's sacrifice had made that possible.

With one final, deep breath, Thorne turned toward the horizon, feeling the warmth of the sun on his back, and took the first step toward the future. There would be pain. There would be loss. But there would also be life. A life lived for love, for Liora, and for the world they had fought to save.

And though the final thorn of their journey had been

sacrificed, the love they shared would continue to bloom, forever.

It would never fade.

Not as long as he remembered.

Not as long as the stars shone in the sky.

Sixteen

The Heart's End

The forest was quiet now, the haunting winds that had once carried the echoes of dark magic now replaced by the soft whispers of the trees. A sense of peace had settled over the land, but it was not the kind of peace that came with ease. No, this peace had been earned—wrought from blood, sacrifice, and the very essence of love itself.

Thorne stood at the edge of the forest, his eyes scanning the horizon where the world had unfolded in front of him, a world that had been both shattered and healed by the events that had transpired. The sun was beginning to set, painting the sky in hues of amber and crimson, a reminder that even the darkest days must eventually end.

He could feel her. Liora.

Her presence lingered in the air, in the soft gusts of wind that stirred the grass at his feet, in the silent call of the birds as they took flight from the trees. The love they had shared was woven into the fabric of the world itself, a bond unbroken by time or death. It was a part of him now, like the blood in his veins.

And yet, there was a weight on his heart, a pull that drew him deeper into himself, deeper into the remnants of their shared journey. The curse had been broken, yes, but its shadows still lingered in his soul.

He closed his eyes, taking a deep breath, letting the scent of the forest fill his lungs. There was no curse now—no dark force that bound them together with threads of magic. It was gone. But that didn't mean the road ahead was without its challenges. The healing that had to take place was not just of the body, but of the heart.

He had learned that much in the time since Liora's sacrifice.

Thorne had spent days, weeks even, walking through the forest, trying to understand what had truly happened. What the curse had meant. Why it had existed in the first place. He had come to realize that it was never truly about the magic. It had always been about them. About their love. About how deeply their hearts had been intertwined, how fate had conspired to shape them, to push them toward the very edge of destruction, only to force them to rise from it.

Liora had given everything to break the curse. She had sacrificed herself so that they could be free. And in doing so, she had revealed the truth. The curse had never been just a spell cast by a vengeful sorcerer or a twist of fate. It had been a part of something older—something more profound.

It was the curse of the heart.

The very thing that had made them who they were had also been their undoing. Their love, their bond, had been both a gift and a burden. And the curse had existed to force them to confront it. To prove that love—true love—could survive even the most unbearable of trials.

But now, with the curse gone, Thorne found himself alone in a world that no longer carried the same weight. His heart was lighter, yes, but it was also fractured. The truth was, no amount of magic could undo what they had lost. The sacrifice Liora had made had freed him, but it had also left a void that could never be filled.

He didn't know how to move forward without her.

Thorne's gaze fell to the ground, and there, at his feet, he saw the faintest glimmer—a trace of magic, no more than a whisper of what had once been. He knelt slowly, his hand brushing over the grass, and as he did, a single flower bloomed at his touch. It was pale violet, its petals soft and delicate, the faintest glow surrounding it.

Liora's flower.

Thorne's heart clenched in his chest as he gazed at the bloom. It was a symbol of everything they had shared—of the love that had carried them through the darkest days of their lives. The flower had been a part of her, a piece of her magic, and it had been born from the very depths of their connection.

But now, as he watched the flower pulse with soft light, he realized something. The magic that had once bound them, that had once been the source of so much pain and suffering, was no longer something that held him captive. It was a part of him, yes, but it was no longer something that could control him.

And yet, in its light, there was a sense of closure. A sense of peace.

He stood up, gently pressing a finger to the delicate petals. A single tear slipped down his cheek, but he didn't wipe it away.

It wasn't a tear of sorrow, but of something else. A bittersweet kind of understanding.

The curse was truly broken. And with it, Liora's sacrifice had been the key to setting him free. But in doing so, she had given him something more than he could ever have imagined. She had given him the chance to live. Not just to survive, but to *live* again.

He could feel her presence in the air, in the very earth beneath his feet. She was there, in the wind, in the leaves. Her love was still with him. But now, it wasn't a weight. It was freedom.

And in that moment, he understood what he had to do.

Liora had freed him from the chains of the curse, but she had also freed him from the prison of his own grief. He would carry her memory with him always. He would carry the love they had shared, even if it was no longer something that lived between them in the same way.

Thorne closed his eyes and took a deep breath, letting the wind carry away the final vestiges of his sorrow. He would never forget her. He would never stop loving her. But he had to live, for her, for the both of them.

"I will always love you," he whispered into the wind, his voice steady, his heart strong. "And I will live for you."

With one last glance at the flower—Liora's flower—he turned and began walking toward the path that led deeper into the forest, toward whatever lay ahead. It was a road he would walk alone, but not without purpose.

For Liora's love had given him everything. And now, he would give it all back to the world.

Far to the east, at the edge of the kingdom, a new dawn was breaking. It was soft, gentle, as if the world itself was waking from a long, dark sleep. The air was fresh with the scent of morning dew, the promise of a new beginning.

And as the sun rose higher in the sky, casting its golden light across the land, there was a sense of calm that settled over the world. The curse was gone. The darkness had been defeated.

And in the heart of the world, the final thorn had been plucked. The last of the pain, the last of the sorrow, had been swept away.

For the first time in a long while, the world felt free.

Liora's sacrifice had been the key to that freedom. And though she was no longer there to walk beside Thorne, her spirit, her love, remained.

Always. Forever.

Thorne walked forward, his steps slow but deliberate, his body carrying the weight of all that had passed, all that had been lost. Each step took him further from the battlefield, further from the pain of the curse that had ruled his life for so long. But though his path led him away from the past, it did not mean he would ever leave it behind.

He would always carry Liora with him.

The forest around him felt different now. Lighter. As if the world had sighed in relief, finally freed from the suffocating grip of darkness. The branches that had once curled inwards, twisting like claws, now stretched upward, as if reaching toward the sky. The ground beneath his boots was soft, no longer trembling with the echoes of ancient magic. Even the air itself was different. It carried the scent of fresh rain, of growing things, of renewal.

The weight of his grief had not left him, but it had shifted. It no longer threatened to break him apart. It had settled into something quieter, something softer. A part of him now, like the scar from an old wound. He had learned to carry it, just as he carried the memory of Liora.

And then, the wind shifted.

For a moment, everything stilled, the trees pausing in their dance, the air holding its breath. And then—he felt it.

A warmth against his skin. A whisper that wasn't quite a voice, yet spoke to the deepest part of his soul.

Thorne…

He stopped walking, his breath catching in his throat. His fingers curled into fists at his sides, the pulse in his veins quickening. He turned his head slightly, listening—waiting.

"Liora?" His voice was barely more than a whisper.

Silence.

But then—movement. A rustling in the leaves, a ripple in the air around him, like the lingering echo of laughter carried on the wind. He knew she was gone, that she had given herself to the magic, to the sacrifice that had saved him, saved them all. But something inside him told him she was still here. Not in body, not in the way he longed for, but in the way that mattered.

The world had changed. The curse was broken. But their love—it remained.

He swallowed hard, his throat tightening. "I wish you were here," he murmured, his fingers grazing the bark of a tree as he passed, feeling the rough texture beneath his fingertips. "I wish I could tell you… I understand now."

The wind picked up again, and in its current, something stirred within him. A memory, not of loss, but of warmth. Of the way she had once looked at him beneath the starlit sky, her eyes filled with quiet determination. Of the way her laughter had melted away even the deepest of his fears.

She had always believed in love. Always believed in the strength of their bond. And in the end, it had been her love that had saved them.

He closed his eyes for a moment, exhaling slowly. "I will not waste this life you gave me, Liora. I swear it."

And with that promise, he pressed forward.

Days passed. Then weeks.

Thorne found himself walking paths he had never taken before, exploring places he had once ignored. The world, once darkened by the shadow of the curse, was now open to him in a way it had never been. He was no longer bound by fate. No longer a prisoner to destiny. He was simply a man, walking forward, one step at a time.

He had left the ruins of the past behind, though the memories would always stay with him. He carried them like a talisman, a reminder of what he had fought for. Of what she had fought for.

One evening, as the sun set low over the horizon, he found himself in a valley filled with wildflowers. They stretched out before him in waves of violet and gold, their petals swaying gently in the breeze. It was the kind of place Liora would have loved. The kind of place where she would have spun in circles with laughter in her eyes, hands reaching out to brush against the flowers as if they held secrets only she could hear.

He knelt down, his fingers grazing one of the blossoms. A soft violet hue. The same color as the magic that had once surrounded her.

A small smile touched his lips. "You would have loved this," he murmured.

The wind stirred, warm against his skin. And for a brief moment, he swore he felt the lightest touch against his shoulder.

A presence. Fleeting, but real.

His heart ached, but it was no longer a pain that consumed him. It was something else now. Something gentler. A bittersweet kind of love, one that would never fade.

He stood, letting the wind carry his breath away with it.

And then, with one last glance at the field of flowers, he turned and walked toward whatever lay ahead.

For the first time in a long, long time, he was truly free.

Seventeen

The Thorn-Bound Heart

The moon hung high in the night sky, its light casting long shadows over the land. The air was crisp, carrying the scent of pine and earth, cool and fresh after the long, dry summer. Thorne walked alone, his boots soft against the path of moss-covered stone that wound through the dense forest. The trees stretched high above him, their branches whispering with the wind as though they carried secrets that only the night could hear.

It had been years since the curse had been broken. Since Liora had made her sacrifice. Since the dark forces that had ruled their lives had finally been driven away. The world was a different place now, brighter in some ways, but also heavier in others. Thorne had come to understand that freedom came not only from breaking the chains that had bound him, but from the weight of the love he had once known. It wasn't just a love that had burned bright. It was a love that had torn him apart, changed him in ways he could never fully explain.

And still, here he was.

Every step he took seemed to pull him deeper into the forest, into the shadows of the past that he could never quite escape. For the love they had shared, for the bond that had once tied them so tightly together, had not truly gone. It remained.

The thorn-bound heart was not just the emblem of the curse that had shaped their fates. It was a reminder of what they had lost and what had endured. It was a symbol of love's power, the power that defied death, that refused to die even when its source was gone. And though Liora was no longer with him, her presence was still felt—like the warmth of the sun after a storm, like the faintest memory of a melody you could never quite remember but always feel in the deepest part of you.

As Thorne made his way deeper into the forest, he reached the clearing where the ancient temple had once stood. It was in ruins now, the stone crumbled, vines winding up the walls like veins, consuming what was left of the place that had seen so much pain and loss. The place where they had fought, where Liora had given everything.

Where he had lost her.

But this time, when he reached the center of the clearing, something was different.

The air felt charged with magic. A force he hadn't felt in years.

He paused, his hand going instinctively to the hilt of his sword. The tension in the air was thick. The hairs on the back of his neck prickled, and his heart raced with the realization that he was no longer alone. His breath caught in his throat as he turned slowly, his eyes scanning the shadows around him.

From the edge of the clearing, a figure stepped forward,

emerging from the darkness like a ghost from another time.

Liora.

For a moment, Thorne's heart stopped, his breath trapped in his chest as he stared at her. It was impossible. She couldn't be here. She was gone. He had buried her memory in the deepest part of his heart, trying to move forward, trying to live without the weight of her loss.

But there she stood, her silhouette outlined by the pale light of the moon. Her form was ethereal, almost translucent, yet unmistakably real. He could see her face, her eyes—the eyes that had once been filled with hope, with the strength of someone who believed in love's power above all else. But now, there was something different in her gaze. Something darker, as if she carried the weight of a thousand years.

Liora didn't speak. She simply stood there, her presence like an anchor in the storm of his emotions. Thorne's legs felt weak beneath him, his heart pounding in his chest as he struggled to breathe. His mind screamed for him to understand what was happening, to make sense of the impossible. But the answer was beyond him.

"Liora?" he breathed, his voice barely a whisper. He stepped toward her, but his feet felt as though they were stuck in the earth, rooted to the ground. The weight of her presence pulled him forward, and yet, a part of him resisted. He had lost her once. He couldn't lose her again.

"Is it really you?" he asked, his voice hoarse with disbelief.

She didn't answer. Instead, she stepped closer, her movements graceful, almost haunting. Her clothes were tattered, but the energy around her was unmistakable. Magic. The kind of magic he hadn't felt in years, the kind that had bound them together in life, in death, and in love.

"Liora," he repeated, his voice shaking now. His hands reached for her, but when he touched her arm, his fingers passed through her, like she was made of smoke.

His breath hitched in his throat as he pulled his hand back, staring at the space where she had been.

"What is this? What's happening?" Thorne whispered. His voice trembled with fear, with grief, with something he couldn't name. "You're gone. I buried you. You… you *died*."

Her eyes softened as she looked at him, and a gentle smile tugged at the corner of her lips. But it was a smile filled with sadness, with the weight of knowledge that he could never understand. She reached up, her hand hovering just in front of his chest, not quite touching him, but somehow, he felt the warmth of her presence surround him, like the faintest kiss of sunlight on a cold morning.

"I'm not here in the way you think, Thorne," her voice was soft, distant, yet it echoed in his mind like the whisper of wind through the trees. "I'm here because of you. Because of what you've become. Because of *us*."

He opened his mouth to speak, but the words didn't come. The realization hit him all at once, and his heart seemed to freeze in his chest. He took a step back, his eyes wide as he processed what she was saying.

"This is… what you wanted?" Thorne asked, his voice trembling. "For me to live without you?"

Liora nodded slowly, her expression pained but filled with understanding. "I wanted you to live, Thorne. I wanted you to live for both of us. The curse is gone. The magic that bound us is no longer a chain. But our hearts… our hearts are still bound by love."

Thorne shook his head, feeling the tightness in his chest

deepen. "I can't live without you. I *don't* know how to live without you." His voice broke, his body shaking with the emotion he couldn't hold back any longer.

Liora stepped closer, her ethereal presence wrapping around him like a balm to his aching soul. "You've already learned how to live, Thorne. You've been living all this time. For me. For us. But the curse, the magic that tied us together—it's not what defines us. It was only a test. A test to see how far we would go for love."

Her words were like a balm, soothing the ache in his heart, but they also left him with a bitter taste on his tongue. He had fought so hard, lost so much, and now—now it seemed like the battle was over. She was gone. And yet, her love for him lingered, still pulsing like a heartbeat, echoing in every corner of his being.

He closed his eyes, trying to pull himself together. "How do I move on, Liora? How do I live knowing you're not here with me?"

Her hand reached up, her fingers brushing against his cheek, but it was not flesh on flesh. It was a warmth, a sensation of something intangible yet profound. She smiled softly at him. "You've already started, Thorne. You've carried me in your heart every day since I left. Now, you must let that love guide you. Live, not for the pain, but for the joy we shared. For the love we created. That is what will carry you forward."

Tears welled in his eyes as he looked at her, his breath catching in his throat. He had never wanted this. He had never wanted to lose her, to carry the weight of a love that could never be fully realized again. But the truth was undeniable. She had been his world, and though she was gone, she had not truly left him.

"I can't forget you," Thorne whispered, his voice breaking as the tears fell. "I don't want to forget you."

"You won't," Liora said softly, her voice steady. "You'll carry me with you. In every breath. In every step. In every choice you make. We are bound, Thorne. Always."

And with that, the last of her presence began to fade. The light that had surrounded her dimmed, slowly disappearing into the night, leaving only the soft rustle of the wind as a reminder that she had been there. That she always would be.

Thorne stood in the clearing, his heart heavy with the weight of love and loss, but also lighter with the knowledge that he had not been abandoned. Liora's love had transcended death, had lived on in the very fabric of the world around him. He would carry that love forward, as she had asked him to.

As the wind whispered through the trees, Thorne closed his eyes one final time, allowing himself to feel the warmth of her love, the strength of their bond, deep within his heart.

And then, slowly, with renewed determination, he turned toward the horizon, the path ahead uncertain but open, knowing that love—true love—would always guide him forward.

The forest around him shifted, as if the very trees had exhaled with the weight of what had just passed. The air no longer hummed with the remnants of magic, and yet, something deeper remained. It wasn't power. It wasn't a lingering curse.

It was love.

Liora was gone, yet she wasn't. She had never truly left. And as Thorne stood there, breathing in the cool night air, he felt it deep in his soul—this was not an ending. It was a beginning.

The realization came slowly, as if his heart had to process what his mind already knew. He had spent years searching for her in the wind, in the rustling of leaves, in the way the stars glowed against the dark sky. But she had been with him all along.

Her voice, though no longer spoken, lived in his memory.

Her laughter, though distant, echoed in the spaces between his thoughts.

Her touch, though no longer tangible, was in the warmth that settled into his bones when he thought of her.

The thorn-bound heart was not a curse. It never had been. It was a mark of love's endurance, of how love was never something to be broken—it merely changed form.

And now, as Thorne took his first step away from the clearing, he understood what Liora had meant.

She had given him life. Not in the way he had once wanted, but in the way he needed. A life that could be lived, not burdened by sorrow, but lifted by the love they had shared. She had always believed that love was stronger than anything else in the world. Stronger than magic. Stronger than death.

Now, he believed it too.

Thorne made his way through the trees, the moonlight guiding his path as it always had. The wind carried the scent of earth and pine, and somewhere in the distance, the faint call of an owl echoed through the silence. The world was still. At peace.

And for the first time in years, so was he.

There was no more battle to fight. No more fate to defy. No more curse to run from.

Now, there was only life. A life that stretched before him like an open road, waiting for him to walk forward. A life that he would live in honor of the love he had lost, and the love that would remain within him for all eternity.

He touched his chest lightly, where the thorns had once bound his heart. There was no longer pain there. Just warmth. A reminder.

He closed his eyes and whispered softly into the night, his voice carried away by the wind.

"I will always love you, Liora."

The trees swayed gently, as if answering him. The wind curled around him, warm and comforting.

And then, as if the world itself had given its blessing, the first light of dawn touched the horizon.

A new day.

A new beginning.

With a quiet breath, Thorne turned his back on the past, on the ruins of what had once been, and stepped into the future.

The thorn-bound heart would always be his, but now, it was no longer a burden.

It was a gift.

A love that had survived beyond time.

And a love that would never fade.

Eighteen

The New Dawn

The first light of the morning broke through the horizon, a faint golden glow creeping across the landscape, spilling over the fields like liquid fire. The world, still wrapped in the remnants of night's cool embrace, stirred with life as the sun began its slow rise. The birds awoke first, their songs filling the air with the promise of a new day. The wind, once chill, began to warm, carrying with it the scent of freshly blossomed flowers and earth damp from the night's dew.

For the first time in years, the land seemed to breathe.

Thorne stood at the edge of the forest, his silhouette outlined by the soft light, the trees behind him stretching tall and proud. His eyes were fixed on the horizon, where the dawn had painted the sky with hues of pink and orange. The landscape was tranquil, quiet, but beneath the surface, something stirred within him—something he couldn't quite name. It was the calm after a storm, the peace that comes only after the battle is fought, after the sacrifice has been made.

But even in the peace, he could feel the absence. Liora's absence. Her absence had become a constant companion, a shadow that walked beside him in every quiet moment. No matter how much time passed, how much the world around him changed, the ache in his heart never quite faded. The love they had shared was forever etched into his soul, and though the curse was gone, its scars remained.

He didn't know if he would ever stop feeling it—her love, her memory, the way she had touched every part of his life. But now, he knew he could live with it.

And so, he walked forward, his steps firm on the earth beneath him. The ground felt solid, unyielding, but in his chest, his heart still beat in rhythm with the promise he had made to her: to live. To carry the love they had shared into the world, even if it meant walking alone.

As Thorne moved deeper into the forest, his hand brushed against the bark of a nearby tree. It was smooth, cool to the touch, but there was a subtle energy to it, something that felt alive, as though the very earth around him had absorbed the magic of the past. He could almost hear the echoes of their battle, the clash of magic, the whispers of their voices as they fought, as they loved, as they struggled to break free from the curse.

And in the quiet moments after, he could still feel the remnants of her touch, the echo of her laughter, the warmth of her smile.

But now, it was time to move forward.

The forest opened before him, revealing a small clearing where the grass grew thick and green, the sunlight spilling through the canopy above. In the center of the clearing stood a small stone fountain, its surface still, reflecting the sky like a mirror. The air was fragrant with the smell of wildflowers, their vibrant colors spilling over the edges of the fountain, and as Thorne stepped closer, he felt the pulse of life around him— he was part of it now. Not just as a man who had survived, but as one who would keep going, who would live for those who could not.

He sank to his knees beside the fountain, running his fingers along the cool stone. His breath was steady, though his heart still pounded with the memories of everything they had shared. Everything they had lost.

But in this moment, there was peace.

A soft rustling in the grass caught his attention. He glanced to his left, his eyes narrowing as the wind shifted, carrying a familiar scent—one that was impossible to ignore. It was subtle, like a trace of perfume lingering in the air, but there was no mistaking it. Liora's presence.

He stood, slowly, feeling the beat of his heart quicken in his chest. The wind swirled around him, tugging at his clothes, whispering in his ears like a secret. He closed his eyes for a moment, inhaling deeply. There was no one here. Not physically. No footsteps, no voice. But something stirred deep within him. A sense of connection he couldn't explain. Something that had always been a part of him—something that, despite all odds, still lingered.

He felt it again, a pulse, soft but undeniable. Liora. It wasn't a vision. It wasn't a dream. It was something else. A presence. A memory. Her love, that thread that had connected them so completely, so irrevocably, still lingered, even in her absence.

The wind died down as quickly as it had come, and with it,

the sensation faded. Thorne's breath caught in his throat as he opened his eyes. The clearing was still, untouched. But inside him, something had shifted. He could still feel her. Still hear the echo of her laughter in his mind, still see the warmth in her eyes. It was as though the world around him had momentarily shifted, reminding him that love had no end. It transcended space, time, even death.

He stood, his fingers lingering on the fountain's stone as he looked up at the sky. The sun had risen higher now, casting golden beams across the field. He could feel the weight of everything they had fought for—the weight of the lives they had changed, the sacrifices they had made. Liora had given everything for him. For them.

He wouldn't waste it.

Thorne turned and began to walk again, stepping lightly through the soft grass, his footsteps quiet, measured. He had a new purpose now. He would carry the love they had shared, the love that had changed the very fabric of his being, into the world. And though it was not the future he had once imagined—one filled with laughter and joy with her by his side—it was the future he had now.

He would build it, step by step.

The days turned into weeks. The weeks into months. Thorne found his way in the world again, though it was never the same as it had been before. The love he had for Liora shaped every decision he made, and though the ache in his heart never fully faded, it became a part of him—woven into the very fiber of his being. It no longer crushed him. It no longer defined him.

It was simply the pulse of his existence.

Far to the east, Liora's name was spoken in the wind, carried across the land to the very edges of the kingdom. Her story had become a legend, a tale of sacrifice and love, told around campfires and in the hushed whispers of the elders. The curse that had once bound them together was gone, but its legacy remained.

And somewhere, in the quiet places of the world, where the magic still lingered, Thorne could feel the connection to her. A bond that could never be severed. No matter how far apart they were.

He had returned to the city eventually, though he no longer carried the title of prince. That life was no longer his. Instead, he had become something else—something more. He had become a leader, a man who knew the value of sacrifice, the weight of love, and the importance of freedom.

His days were filled with work, with rebuilding what had been lost, with helping the people of the kingdom find peace after the long years of war and darkness. But every night, when the stars shone above him, when the wind whispered through the trees, he would pause, his heart still remembering the love that had once been.

He would smile then, softly, his eyes reflecting the glow of the stars. He would smile for her.

And as the years passed, Thorne found peace in knowing that Liora's love would never fade. It had become part of the world, part of the fabric of the earth itself. Her sacrifice had broken the curse, yes, but it had also created something new. A future. A future that would be lived with the memory of her, always.

He could never return to her. But he didn't have to.

For the love they had shared, the bond they had forged, would never truly be severed. It had transcended everything—

time, death, and distance. It had become the foundation of his life. And in that, he found the greatest gift of all.

Hope for the future.

And the knowledge that love—true love—was never lost.

It was eternal.

As the years passed, Thorne continued to walk the path he had set for himself—one paved with memories of Liora and the love they had shared. The world around him seemed to evolve with each passing season, yet there were moments when it all stood still, as if waiting for him to catch up. The quiet nights, when the moon hung low and the stars glittered with a cold, indifferent brilliance, brought with them the most bittersweet of reflections.

Liora's absence was still a shadow that loomed over him, but it had become something different over time. It was no longer just sorrow. It had transformed into something more enduring—respect, perhaps, or reverence. Her love had shaped him in ways he could not have imagined when he first stood on the battlefield, grasping at whatever fragments of hope he could find. She had taught him that love was not something that could be kept for oneself. It was meant to be given freely, without expectation, without thought of the cost.

He had learned that lesson the hardest way.

The kingdom was at peace now, but peace—true peace—was a delicate thing. Thorne had spent his days rebuilding, helping the people recover from the wounds of war, of fear, of long years under the shadow of the curse. He had found a new purpose, and in that purpose, he had found healing. He still often found himself walking alone in the fields, in the forests, where the wildflowers bloomed in soft bursts of violet and gold, where the scent of pine and moss filled the air.

But even as the seasons shifted and the world changed, Thorne knew that there was always a part of him that remained with Liora. It was a place in his heart, a soft corner where her memory lived, untouchable by time. She was gone, yes, but she was never lost.

On this night, as the cold autumn wind swept through the open field, Thorne stood by a small river, its surface glistening under the pale light of the waxing moon. He had come here many times, alone, to think. The water seemed to carry the weight of his thoughts, its flow steady and unyielding. The ripples, small but constant, felt like a mirror of his own heart—ever moving, ever changing, yet anchored by something deeper.

He leaned against a weathered stone, his gaze fixed on the stars above, those silent witnesses to his life, to all that had passed, to everything that was yet to come.

The sound of footsteps broke the stillness of the night, faint at first, then closer. Thorne stiffened, turning slowly. For a moment, his heart skipped a beat, as the faintest scent of wildflowers—the same flowers that had bloomed at the edge of the old temple—seemed to hang in the air around him.

He blinked, as if trying to clear his senses, and when his eyes met the figure standing a few paces away from him, his breath caught in his throat.

Liora.

It couldn't be. It was impossible.

Yet there she stood, her silhouette framed by the pale moonlight, her form glowing with an ethereal radiance that seemed to make the very world shift around her. Her hair, once tangled and wild, now fell in waves of silver, catching the light like strands of stardust. Her eyes, once full of hope and joy, were now soft with something deeper—an understanding, a peace that transcended time.

Her gaze met his, steady, unflinching, and for a moment, Thorne could do nothing but stare, his heart pounding in his chest.

"You… you're not real," he whispered, the words barely audible.

Liora's lips curled into a small, sad smile, the same smile that had once melted all of his doubts and fears. The smile that had been the light of his life.

"I'm as real as your love for me, Thorne," she said softly, her voice the same, yet somehow different. There was no confusion, no sorrow in her tone. It was calm, resolute. "I am here because of you. Because of what we were, what we will always be."

Thorne's mind raced. His heart seemed to flutter and crash at the same time. "But you're… gone. I buried you, Liora. You died. You gave yourself for me."

Her smile deepened, though there was sorrow in it. "I gave everything to break the curse, yes. But in doing so, I left behind a part of myself. A part that will always be with you. And you, Thorne—your love, your heart—will always carry me. You must know that."

"I know." Thorne's voice broke as he took a step closer to her. "But I can't keep living like this. I can't keep carrying you when you're no longer here. I can't do it anymore."

Liora took a step forward, her hand reaching out to him, but stopping just short of touching his chest. "You can. You must. Because you still live, Thorne. You still have time. Time to do everything we dreamed of, together, in another way."

Thorne felt the words hit him like a weight, sinking deep into his chest. "I've tried to move on. I've tried to live. But how can I, when you're still here? When everything reminds me of you? Every time I close my eyes, every time I breathe, it's you. Your love. Your loss."

Her eyes softened as she gazed at him, understanding the depth of his pain. "I never wanted to cause you suffering, Thorne. I never wanted you to hurt like this. But I wanted you to live. For both of us. For everything we were. And everything we still are."

"But you're..." He swallowed hard, unable to finish the sentence.

She shook her head gently, stepping closer, her form more solid now, as if she were becoming real again in some way, but still not quite human. Not fully there.

"You've already begun the hardest part of your journey. You've learned to carry the love we shared, and now, it's time for you to share it. With the world. With yourself. You cannot keep holding onto the past. It is time to let it go, Thorne."

The words cut through him like a blade, leaving a jagged emptiness in their wake. He could feel her, still, in every inch of his being. But as she spoke, he knew, in that deep place inside of him that he had kept hidden for so long, that she was right.

He had been carrying her memory as if it were a weight, thinking that it was something to mourn. But Liora hadn't wanted that. She hadn't wanted him to drown in grief. She wanted him to live. To find peace in the love they had shared, to build a future that honored what they had built together, even if they could never be together again in the same way.

Thorne's breath shook as he nodded, his chest heavy, but his heart filled with an odd sense of clarity.

"I will," he said softly. "I will let go of the pain."

Liora's smile deepened, her face glowing with love. "Good. Because, Thorne, the world still needs you. And in your heart, I will always be with you. You won't ever be alone."

And then, as softly as she had appeared, she faded. Her form became light, flickering like a flame, then dissipating into the night. The wind picked up again, the air cool and crisp, and the faintest scent of wildflowers lingered for a moment before vanishing entirely.

Thorne stood alone in the clearing once more, but this time, he didn't feel the emptiness that had consumed him for so long. He didn't feel the weight of his grief bearing down on him. Instead, he felt lighter. The burden of loss was still there, but it was no longer suffocating him. The love they had shared, that bond they had built, would always be with him. He could carry it, cherish it, and still move forward. He could honor her by living, by doing everything she had hoped he would.

He turned back toward the path, his footsteps firm, steady. The night was still, but it no longer felt cold. The stars above shimmered in a new light, one that spoke of hope. The dawn was breaking, and though Liora was no longer by his side, her love would continue to guide him.

The future was his to shape. The love they shared, bound together by time and magic, would live on in every step he took.

And for the first time in a long time, Thorne knew—*he was ready*.

The new dawn had arrived.

Nineteen

The Legacy of the Thorn

The wind whispered through the trees, carrying with it the sound of rustling leaves, soft and rhythmic like a lullaby. The sun was low in the sky, casting a golden hue over the forest. The leaves were turning with the change of season, hues of amber and crimson dancing in the breeze. It was a time of renewal, of quiet reflection. The air was crisp with the promise of change.

Thorne stood on the edge of the clearing, watching as the world continued to shift and change around him. The kingdom was at peace now, the land quiet and unburdened by the curse that had once shadowed their lives. And yet, there was something that still clung to him. Something that would never fade.

He could feel it in the earth beneath his feet. The legacy of their love.

It had been years since Liora's sacrifice. Years since the curse had been lifted. But their love, their bond, had transcended time and death. It had become more than a memory—it had become a force that shaped the world in ways Thorne couldn't yet understand.

He had traveled far from the kingdom, had ventured into distant lands, seeking new horizons, new experiences. But there were days when the weight of the past would find him, when the memory of Liora's face, her smile, would come rushing back with an intensity that took his breath away. Those moments were both painful and beautiful, a reminder of all they had been, and of all they could never have.

But even in those moments of sorrow, Thorne knew that he was not alone. Not truly. Her love was with him. In the wind. In the stillness of the forests. In the quiet moments when the world felt as if it had stopped turning. And it was in the hearts of the people whose lives they had touched.

In the town that Thorne had helped rebuild, there was a small tavern that had become a gathering place for the people—young and old, rich and poor. It was here, in the warmth of the firelight and the hum of conversation, that the story of Liora and Thorne had begun to take root. It was a tale passed down from the elders to the children, a legend whispered in hushed tones on stormy nights, a story that spoke of love's power to overcome even the darkest forces.

It was the story of the thorn-bound heart.

"Did you hear the tale of the prince and the healer?" a young woman asked as she sat at the bar, her eyes wide with excitement. She leaned forward, her voice dropping to a conspiratorial whisper. "The one who broke the curse, the one who saved us all?"

The tavern went quiet at the mention of the tale, the familiar hush that followed every time the story was told. The air grew thick with anticipation, the flicker of the firelight casting shadows on the faces of the listeners.

"Aye," an older man replied from the corner, his voice gruff but filled with reverence. "I heard it from my grandmother. The healer, Liora—she was no ordinary woman. She had magic in her veins, magic that could heal the broken and the sick. But it wasn't just that. She had a heart so full of love that it could tear down mountains. And the prince, Thorne—he was cursed, bound to destroy the one he loved. But their love was stronger than the curse. Stronger than any magic."

"Stronger than death?" the young woman asked, her voice tinged with disbelief.

"Aye," the old man nodded, taking a slow sip from his mug. "They fought the curse together, broke it with their love. But not without a cost. She gave everything for him. She died to break the curse. And he… he lived on. But her love—her spirit—it never left him. Not for a moment."

The young woman leaned back, her eyes wide, captivated by the story. "What happened to the prince? What did he do after?"

The old man smiled, a soft, knowing smile. "He lived. He built. He loved. He carried her with him, in his heart, every day. And in the end, he became more than just a prince. He became a legend, a man who knew that love was the greatest magic of all."

Thorne had often wondered what the world would say about him when he was gone. He had never expected to be remembered, not like this. His name, his story, it had passed from the lips of the elders to the next generation, carried like a flame that refused to die.

It was strange to hear the tales. Strange to hear people speak of him as a legend. Of Liora. Their love, their sacrifice—it had become something more than just a story. It had become a part of the kingdom's history, a symbol of hope, of resilience. And though the pain of her loss still lingered within him, he found comfort in the fact that they had left something behind. Something that would outlast them both.

One evening, as the sun began to set and the air turned cooler, Thorne made his way through the village. He had been here many times, walking the familiar streets, seeing the faces of those who had been touched by the love he and Liora had shared. But tonight felt different. The weight of the past hung heavily in the air. The world felt on the verge of something. And Thorne could feel it in his bones.

He passed by the tavern, where the flickering light from the windows spilled out into the street, casting shadows on the cobblestones. Inside, the murmurs of conversation grew louder as people gathered to share the tale of the thorn-bound heart once again. Thorne stood for a moment, watching from the doorway, before he stepped inside.

The room fell silent when they saw him, the legend himself, standing at the threshold. He had grown older, his once-dark hair now streaked with silver, his face marked by the passage of time. But his eyes—his eyes were the same. The same deep green that had once held the gaze of a young healer, full of promise and love. He was a man who had lived a life he never thought possible, a life forged by the power of love and sacrifice.

Thorne raised a hand in greeting, a small smile on his lips. "Good evening," he said softly, his voice steady but carrying the weight of a thousand untold stories.

The silence hung for only a moment before the old man from the corner raised his mug in the air. "To Thorne," he said, his voice filled with reverence. "The one who broke the curse. The one who lived for love."

The room echoed with murmurs of agreement, the people of the village lifting their glasses in honor of the man who had changed their lives. The young woman from earlier stood, a smile on her face as she approached him.

"Thorne," she said softly, her voice filled with awe. "I've heard the stories… but to see you, to speak with you. It's more than I ever imagined."

Thorne's smile softened as he placed a hand on her shoulder. "The stories are just that," he said quietly. "Stories. What matters is what we do with the time we have. What matters is the love we share."

The young woman nodded, her eyes bright with tears. "You and Liora… you showed us that love can overcome anything. That even the greatest darkness can be defeated with love. It's a legacy that will never be forgotten."

Thorne's heart swelled with a quiet pride. "It's a legacy I never wanted. But it's one that's mine now. And it's one that I hope will inspire others. Love isn't always easy. But it's worth it."

He turned to the crowd, his gaze sweeping over the faces that looked back at him with admiration, with respect, and with hope. For a brief moment, it felt as though time itself had stopped, as if the entire world was holding its breath.

"Liora and I," Thorne said, his voice filled with a deep emotion that he could no longer suppress. "We didn't have forever. But the love we shared was enough. Enough to break the curse, enough to free us both. And now, I want you all to remember that. To live with that love in your hearts, no matter what happens."

A hush fell over the room, and for a long moment, no one spoke. But then, the young woman smiled softly, her eyes filled with understanding. "We will, Thorne. We will."

And with those words, the room erupted in applause, the sound echoing in the walls of the tavern, reverberating through the village, through the kingdom, and beyond. Thorne stood there, surrounded by the warmth of their love, their respect, and their gratitude.

In that moment, he understood what Liora had wanted for him, for them both. They had broken the curse. They had lived, and now, they had left a legacy that would endure long after they were gone.

The thorn-bound heart was not just a symbol of pain and sacrifice. It was a symbol of love's eternal power. And it would never fade.

And as the night stretched on, Thorne smiled, knowing that the love they had shared would live on, in the hearts of all those who believed in its power.

The legacy of the thorn would always endure.

The applause lingered, soft and steady, as if the room itself could not quite bring itself to let go of the moment. Thorne stood in the center of it all, his heart swelling, but his mind still a place of quiet reflection. He had always feared that Liora's memory would fade, that their love would be lost in the shadows of time. But tonight, standing in the midst of those who still carried their story, he realized that fear had been unfounded. Their love had not just been a passing thing; it was a legacy, woven into the very fabric of the world.

As the murmurs of conversation resumed around him, Thorne found himself lost in thought. The past had shaped him, no doubt. But so had the present. The people, the land, the life he was building—everything was a reflection of what he and Liora had done, what they had given to each other. It was in the way the kingdom had healed, in the way the people had begun to live without fear, without the weight of a curse hanging over their heads.

The young woman, still standing near him, watched him with wide eyes, perhaps sensing that his mind had drifted away from the celebration.

"Is there… anything you regret?" she asked tentatively, her voice quiet yet filled with an earnestness that made Thorne pause.

He turned to look at her, his gaze softening. She was young, eager, filled with the kind of hope that had once burned brightly in his own heart. A part of him longed to tell her all the ways love had betrayed him, all the ways he had been broken by it, but that wouldn't be fair to her. It wouldn't be fair to the world that had learned to believe in the kind of love he and Liora had shared.

"No," he said simply, his voice steady. "I don't regret a single thing. Love isn't something you regret. Not when it's real."

The young woman smiled, a small spark of something bright in her eyes. She nodded, her shoulders relaxing as if she had been waiting for those words. They weren't the answers she had expected, perhaps, but they were the truth.

Thorne's thoughts drifted again, this time to the quiet evenings when he would walk alone in the fields, surrounded by the soft, gentle hum of nature. There, in the stillness, he had often found Liora's presence. Not in the way one might expect, not in any physical form, but in the breeze that would blow through the trees, in the moonlight that would bathe him in a soft glow. It was as though her spirit had become part of the land itself, a reminder that no matter how far apart they had been, they would always be connected.

He stepped away from the young woman and toward the large window at the far end of the tavern. The view outside revealed the moon hanging low in the sky, its pale light casting long shadows over the village. The wind had picked up again, rustling the leaves on the trees just beyond the cobblestone path. The air was thick with the promise of something new.

He didn't realize that he was speaking aloud until the words escaped him. "I sometimes wonder… what she would say if she were here now. How would she look at all of this?"

The silence in the tavern deepened at his words. The fire crackled softly behind him, its warmth filling the room, but it was the soft murmur of the villagers that reached him. He didn't need to turn around to know that they, too, were reflecting on the significance of what had just been said. It wasn't just about the love he and Liora had shared. It was about the future—their legacy, and what it would mean for those who came after them.

He smiled softly to himself, the corners of his lips pulling up in a quiet, wistful grin. *What would she say?*

Liora would have been proud. Proud of the way the kingdom had recovered, of the way the people had stood together, united in their shared belief that love could heal even the deepest of wounds. She had always believed that love was more than just a feeling—it was a force, a power that could change the world if given the chance. And in the end, her love had done exactly that.

He sighed, leaning against the wooden frame of the window, his eyes fixed on the moonlit path before him. It seemed so simple now, the life they had built—the peace, the hope, the quiet legacy of love that lingered in the air like the softest of whispers. They had never asked for glory, never sought to be remembered. But in the end, their love had written itself into the hearts of all who believed in its power.

In the far corner of the room, an older woman raised her glass, her voice carrying through the quiet tavern. "To Liora, the healer, and to Thorne, the prince who loved her."

The murmurs of agreement spread like ripples across the room. Thorne turned slowly, his heart fluttering at the mention of her name. He had not forgotten. He would never forget.

"To love," he said softly, his voice carrying across the room. "To love that never ends."

The room echoed with the clink of glasses, the sound of celebration, but in that moment, Thorne's mind drifted once more to the silent places where their love had been born. The wildflowers in the fields, the soft brush of the wind, the moonlight that always seemed to shine a little brighter when he needed it most.

Liora was everywhere.

The night stretched on, filled with laughter and song, but as Thorne stood in the midst of it, he could feel the weight of everything they had created. He knew that the legacy of their love would continue to grow, to inspire, to touch the lives of others, for generations to come. The tale of the thorn-bound heart would live on, not as a tragic story, but as a reminder of the power of love, its ability to transcend time, to break curses, to heal.

In the quiet moments, when the world became still, Thorne could still feel Liora beside him. Not in body, but in spirit, in heart. They were bound together still, as they always would be, by something more enduring than magic, more lasting than time itself.

As the last of the evening's celebrations came to a close and the villagers began to filter out, Thorne lingered by the window, his fingers brushing the cool stone of the wall. He looked out at the darkened horizon, where the first light of dawn was beginning to emerge, casting its soft glow over the world.

And in that moment, with the promise of a new day on the horizon, he knew that love—true love—never truly ends. It becomes part of the world. It lives on in the stories we tell, in the lives we touch, in the hearts that remain open to its power.

As the first rays of the sun broke through the trees, Thorne took a deep breath, letting the warmth fill him. The legacy of the thorn was not one of suffering, not one of pain, but of something more. It was a legacy of love's enduring strength. And he would carry that legacy with him, always.

And so, as the dawn broke, a new day began—one where the past would live on, but the future was all his to shape.

The legacy of the thorn, of Liora, and of their love, would endure forever.

Twenty

The End of the Curse

The winds shifted with the fall of dusk, stirring the tall grass that stretched across the open plains. The air was thick with the promise of change, of something ancient finally being laid to rest. The moon hung low in the sky, casting its silvery light across the earth, as if it were watching over everything—over all that had happened, and all that was yet to come. The land seemed to pulse with a quiet, steady rhythm, as though it were waiting for a final resolution, an end to the story that had begun so many years ago.

In the far distance, the ruins of the ancient temple loomed like a shadow. The place where everything had started. Where the curse had been born, where love had been tested beyond its limits. Liora and Thorne's tale had been shaped by this place, by the very magic that had bound their fates together, and though the curse had long since been broken, the lingering questions remained unanswered. Questions that had haunted

Thorne for years.

He had spent so many years searching for answers, digging through the ruins of the past, trying to understand the nature of the curse that had bound him to Liora, trying to uncover the truth behind the dark magic that had threatened to tear them apart. The answers had always eluded him—until now.

Tonight, the mystery would be revealed.

Thorne stood at the threshold of the temple, the wind howling through the shattered walls, its mournful cries echoing in the stillness. The air around him was thick with magic, a palpable energy that seemed to thrum in his chest, drawing him closer to the heart of the temple. The place where it had all begun. Where it would all end.

He took a step forward, his boots crunching on the rubble that littered the ground. His heart beat with a heavy rhythm, the weight of the years pressing down on him. Every step seemed to echo in the vast emptiness of the temple, a place once filled with magic and power, now crumbling and abandoned. And yet, despite its ruin, the air still hummed with energy, with the remnants of something ancient.

As Thorne moved deeper into the temple, he could feel it. The magic. The power that had once held him captive. It was here, still, like a ghost lingering in the dark corners of the world, waiting for its moment to strike. He had come to understand, in the years since Liora's sacrifice, that the curse wasn't just a force of destruction—it was a force of creation, too. It had been born from something older, something deeper than either he or Liora had ever known. And now, it was time to uncover its origins.

At the center of the temple, in the ruins of what had once been the grand altar, there was a large stone slab. Covered in moss and dirt, it seemed like just another forgotten relic of a time long past. But Thorne knew that it held the answers he had been searching for. The answers to the mystery of the curse.

He knelt before the stone, brushing the dirt away, revealing intricate symbols carved into its surface. Symbols that were foreign to him, but familiar in a way he couldn't quite explain. They seemed to pulse with an energy all their own, as if they were waiting for something to awaken them.

His fingers traced the symbols, feeling the power in them. The same power that had once bound him to Liora. The same power that had twisted their fates together, forcing them to sacrifice everything in order to survive. And as he touched the stone, a low hum filled the air, a vibration that seemed to travel through his bones, through his very soul.

He pulled his hand back, his heart racing. The air around him thickened, the magic rising in intensity. Thorne stood slowly, his eyes fixed on the stone, watching as the symbols began to glow with a faint, golden light.

And then, the voice came.

It was a whisper at first, faint and distant, like a breath on the wind. But it grew louder, more insistent, until it filled the temple, echoing in every corner, in every crack of the crumbling walls.

"Thorne…"

His breath caught in his throat. The voice was familiar—soft, gentle, yet filled with an undeniable power. It was Liora.

"Liora," he whispered, his voice trembling. "Where are you?"

The light from the stone pulsed again, and the air seemed to shift, becoming heavy with the weight of history, with the weight of everything that had happened. The ground beneath

Thorne's feet trembled, and the voice grew louder.

"Thorne… I am here. I have always been here."

His heart hammered in his chest, and he stepped back, his eyes wide. The temple around him seemed to pulse with the rhythm of Liora's voice, as though her presence had never truly left. It was not just a memory. Not just a figment of his imagination. She was here. In the magic. In the very fabric of the world they had fought to save.

"Liora…" he said again, his voice desperate. "How? How can this be?"

The light from the stone flared bright, and the air seemed to crackle with energy. The ground shook beneath his feet, and Thorne stumbled, reaching out for support. The voice was stronger now, more solid, as if it were rising from the depths of the earth itself.

"The curse," the voice said. "The curse was never truly about us, Thorne. It was never about you and me. It was about the balance. The balance of power. The balance between light and dark. It was a test, Thorne. A test of love. A test of strength. Of heart. It was designed to shape us, to shape the world."

Thorne's mind raced, his thoughts struggling to keep up with the torrent of words. "The curse… a test?" His voice was hoarse, his mind spinning. "But it was meant to destroy us. To tear us apart. To destroy everything."

"Yes," Liora's voice answered. "But destruction is not always the end. It is a beginning. Love, true love, is the force that binds the world together. It is the force that shapes destiny. And in breaking the curse, in giving everything for one another, you and I proved that love is stronger than any magic. Stronger than any curse."

Thorne's chest tightened. He felt the weight of her words,

the depth of what she was saying. "But what about you? What about your sacrifice?"

There was a pause, and then Liora's voice, soft and full of sorrow, replied, "My sacrifice was not for nothing, Thorne. It was for the world. For the future. For everything we could not have. Our love, though tragic, has shaped the world. It has changed the course of magic. It has altered destiny."

The temple around Thorne seemed to shake again, the walls crumbling more, but the stone beneath him remained steady. The symbols on the slab pulsed, their light growing brighter, as if the magic of the curse had finally reached its peak.

"The curse was never just a punishment," Liora's voice continued. "It was a test of what true love can overcome. What it can endure. And now… now it is finished. The curse has been undone. But love, love will remain."

The temple shook violently, the air crackling with the final release of magic. Thorne stumbled again, his heart racing. The stone beneath him glowed brighter, the energy from it surging through the ground, through the very air around him.

And then, as quickly as it had come, it was over. The light from the stone faded, leaving only the echo of Liora's voice.

"Live, Thorne. Live for both of us. You are free."

Thorne stood in the silence that followed, his breath ragged, his heart pounding in his chest. The air around him was still. The energy had dissipated, but the weight of the moment remained. He had always known the curse had been more than it seemed. He had always known that love was at the heart of it. But hearing Liora's voice, hearing her explain the truth—it had shattered everything he thought he knew.

The curse had been a test, yes, but it had been more. It had been a trial to prove that love could overcome anything. That love, no matter the cost, could alter the course of magic and destiny. And in the end, Liora's sacrifice, their love, had proven it.

The ruins around him seemed to grow still, the air heavy with the remnants of the magic that had once bound him and Liora together. He took a deep breath, the realization settling in his chest.

Liora was gone, but her love—*their* love—would remain, a force that would continue to shape the world. The curse was truly over. And in its place, a new dawn had arrived.

Thorne walked slowly toward the stone slab, kneeling before it once more. The symbols were dim now, but they had not disappeared. They had been a part of him, of her, of them. They were a part of the legacy they had created.

As he stood, he turned toward the open sky, the stars now shining down on him like a thousand silent witnesses. And in that moment, he understood.

Love had triumphed.

The curse was broken, but its legacy would live on forever.

Thorne stood still for a long moment, the echoes of the past swirling around him. The night sky above was a canvas of glittering stars, their light piercing the dark expanse. He had been to the edge of despair, had fought the greatest of battles—against the curse, against destiny itself—but standing there, alone in the ruins of the temple, he felt something he hadn't felt in so long: peace.

The curse had been broken, and with it, the heavy weight that had shackled him for years. He could feel the love he and Liora had shared, still strong, still vibrant within him, but no longer burdened by the magic that had once twisted their fates.

It was now a quiet force—a memory that shaped him, yes, but also a love that had become part of the very world around him.

Thorne took a deep breath, the crisp night air filling his lungs. His heart, though heavy with the memories of all that he had lost, was lighter than it had ever been. It wasn't that he no longer missed her. He always would. But the pain had been transformed into something else—a soft, abiding grief that he could carry without it breaking him. And more than that, it was a love that would never fade, never diminish.

The ruins of the temple stood around him, ancient and forgotten, but no longer holding the darkness they once had. The air felt different—freer, lighter. The world was not without its scars, but the curse that had tainted it had been washed away. And in its place, new growth would come. Life, not just for Thorne, but for all those who would follow in their footsteps.

He turned, the wind brushing against his face, his eyes searching the night for something—anything—that might hold him to the past. But there was nothing. Nothing except the memories of the love that had once been, and would always be, a part of him.

A sound, soft and barely perceptible, reached his ears, and he froze. For a moment, he thought he was imagining it, but then it came again—clearer this time. The soft rustling of leaves, a whisper in the wind. The sound was not unfamiliar. He had heard it before, many times. The breeze that carried it was filled with an unmistakable warmth, like the touch of a hand, gentle but constant. A part of him had always known, had always *felt* it.

"Liora," he whispered, his voice almost lost in the wind.

The sound of her name seemed to fill the air, and for a brief moment, the temple around him faded. The ruins disappeared, the shadows and the darkness of the past receding into the light. It was as if the world was breathing again, as if the land itself had come to life in a new way. He could feel her presence—soft, familiar, eternal—surrounding him, not as a ghost or memory, but as something living, something that lived within him, within the world, within the very fabric of reality.

And with it came the certainty that he wasn't alone. Not truly. Not ever again.

Thorne's eyes closed as he stood there, letting the wind wash over him, his heart swelling with a quiet, final acceptance. He had always feared that he would be lost without her, that her absence would break him. But now, standing in the quiet ruins, he knew that wasn't true. She was with him, always. Her love was with him.

The air around him stilled. The whispers of the wind faded into the night, leaving only the soft sounds of the forest. The earth, the trees, the stars above—everything seemed to hold its breath. Thorne opened his eyes once more, his gaze drawn to the horizon, to the faintest sliver of dawn that began to break at the edge of the world. A new day was coming.

He turned toward it, stepping away from the ruins, away from the past, but not without carrying its lessons. Not without carrying the love that had defined him, that had defined them both. He walked with purpose now, knowing that his journey was not over. He had lived for Liora. He had loved for her. But now, he would live for himself—for the future they had dreamed of, even if that future was one he would face alone.

And as the first light of dawn touched the earth, spilling across the fields like liquid gold, Thorne knew that it was time to leave the shadows behind. It was time to step into the future.

The legacy of the thorn, the legacy of their love, would continue to grow—quietly, steadily—through every life touched by it. It would inspire the hearts of others, reminding them that love, no matter the cost, would always find a way.

Thorne took a final, steady breath as he stepped forward, his steps confident and sure. The past was no longer a weight. It was a part of him, but it did not define him. And as he walked toward the rising sun, he knew that the curse was truly gone. There was no more darkness to fear.

There was only light.

The light of love. The light of hope.

And a future where the legacy of the thorn would never fade.

And so, the tale of Liora and Thorne became a legend—a story passed down through generations, a timeless reminder that love, no matter the cost, would always find a way. Their bond, forged in the fires of sacrifice and tested by fate, lived on in the hearts of those who believed in its power.

Though the curse was gone, the love that had defeated it would remain forever, etched in the very fabric of the world, a legacy for all time.

9 7870 7976 8918